This is Judaism

Michael Keene

Stanley Thornes (Publishers) Ltd

First published in 1996 by:
Stanley Thornes (Publishers) Ltd
Delta Place
27 Bath Road
CHELTENHAM
GL53 7TH
United Kingdom

05   /   10   9   8   7

A catalogue record of this book is available from the British Library.

ISBN 0-7487-2557-1

Printed and bound in China by Midas

Acknowledgements

With thanks to the following for permission to reproduce photographs and illustrations:

ASAP 6, 14, 32, 35, 52, 57, 65, 71, 86, 89, 90, 94 ● Circa 37 (right), 50, 64, 74, 91, 92 ● Chris Fairclough Colour Library 42, 82, 83 ● E Kahn, Jews' College, London 66 ● Rex Features 7 (right), 17, 21, 22 (Sipa Press), 43 (Sipa Press), 47, 69 ● Sonia Halliday Photographs 16 ● Hulton Getty Picture Collection Ltd 20 ● Hutchison Library 7, 41, 46, 72, 95 ● Alex Keene/ Jo MacLennan, The Walking Camera 4, 5, 18, 23, 24, 26, 27, 29, 30, 31, 33, 37, 38, 39, 40, 44, 45, 48, 49 (all), 54 (both), 55, 56, 60, 61, 62, 63, 70, 75, 76, 77 (both), 79, 85, 87 ● Michael Keene 19 ● Network Photographers 59 ● Panos Pictures 51 ● United Reform Synagogue 67 (Mark Henry Photography).

Every effort has been made to contact copyright holders and we apologise if any have been inadvertently overlooked.

Designed by Janet McCallum.

Illustrated by Barking Dog Art, Gillian Hunt.

Cover artwork by Ian Kennedy.

Picture research by Julia Hanson.

Notes

1 Most of the Jews in this country who practise their religion belong to Orthodox synagogues. These are synagogues which follow the traditional Jewish way of life and worship. A much smaller number of Jews belong to Reform or Liberal synagogues. These synagogues do not follow all of the traditional practices. In this book the text and the photographs are largely drawn from the Orthodox tradition.

2 In this book the abbreviations BCE (Before Common Era) and CE (Common Era) are used instead of BC and AD. However, in practice, they mean exactly the same.

3 All quotations in this book are taken from *The Tenakh: The Holy New JPS Translation According to the Traditional Hebrew Text*, published by the Jewish Publication Society, Philadelphia and Jerusalem, 1985.

Contents

Introducing the Jews
Who are the Jews?

The **Jews** have a very long history. It goes back at least 4000 years. During this time they have lived in their own country – **Israel** – but have lost it more than once. They have been scattered throughout the world. They have been slaves and have been killed in their millions. In 1948, when they returned to live in Israel, many Jews thought that it was a miracle.

The Jewish story began with a tribe of nomads called **Hebrews**. They became known much later as **Israelites** (or the 'Children of Israel'). They took this name from one of their early leaders, Jacob, who was renamed '**Israel**'. The later name Jews comes from Judah, the fourth son of Jacob.

The early names of Hebrews and Israelites have been very important for the Jews because:

- **Hebrew** is the language in which the Jewish **Scriptures** were written and which is still spoken by Jews today. **Synagogue** services are conducted in Hebrew.

- Israel was the name given to the land which God promised to the Israelites after they escaped from slavery in Egypt. Israel was originally known as Canaan but to the Israelites it was known as the 'Promised Land'. They conquered the territory gradually and you will find out much more about that on pages 10–13.

Judaism

Judaism is one of the most important religions in the world. It is also a very distinctive religion. In particular, this is because of:

- the Jewish belief in one God. The Jewish Scriptures teach that this God created the world and everything in it before making himself known to **Abraham** and **Moses**. The history of these encounters and what happened next are found in the Jewish Scriptures – especially the **Torah**.

- the Jewish way of life. A Jew is someone who has a Jewish mother. He or she can live anywhere in the world. Many Jews live in Israel, although not everyone in Israel is a Jew. More Jews live elsewhere in the world than in Israel. About 350 000 Jews live in the UK.

All Jews share in the history of their people. Most of them follow a way of life that is based on their faith in God. Some, however, do not do this, although they are proud to count themselves as part of the Jewish 'family'. You might find that a little difficult to understand! All will be explained on pages 10–13.

- What is a Jew?
- What is distinctive about the Jewish belief in God?
- Where are Jews to be found in today's world?

Almost all Jews see themselves as belonging to a large, worldwide 'family' – the family of Jews.

Abraham was one of the founders of the Jewish nation. His story is found in the book of Genesis.

Hebrew is the language in which the Jewish Scriptures are written, and in which synagogue services are conducted.

The **Hebrews** (meaning 'those who passed over the river') were the tribe from which the first Jews grew.

Israel (meaning 'one who stuggled with God') was the name given by God to Jacob. We are told in the Jewish Scriptures that he wrestled all night with God.

The **Israelites** were the group of people who became slaves in Egypt, and who were eventually led out of Egypt by Moses (the Exodus).

A **Jew** is a man or a woman who is born into a Jewish family.

Judaism is the beliefs and worship of the Jewish people.

Moses was a key figure in the history of the Jewish people. He led the Israelites out of Egyptian slavery, and gave them their laws from God.

The Jewish **Scriptures** are the books in the Tenakh, the Jewish Bible.

A **synagogue** is a Jewish place of worship. The word means 'coming together'. The synagogue is also used as a community centre.

The **Torah** (meaning 'teaching') is the most important part of the Jewish Scriptures, containing laws and history. It refers to the first five books – Genesis, Exodus, Leviticus, Deuteronomy and Numbers.

1 a What are the characteristics of a family?
 b Why do you think that being a Jew is often likened to belonging to a family?

2 This photograph shows the inside of a synagogue, a Jewish place of worship.
a Who were the Hebrews and Israelites?
b Why are they now called Jews?
c What is it that all Jews share?

What does it mean to be a Jew?

A person is a Jew because he or she has a Jewish mother. It is that, and nothing else, that makes a person a Jew. Being born into a Jewish family, however, gives a person a special link with other Jews – with those who have long since died and with those who are scattered throughout the world today. The link that binds Jew to Jew is as strong today as it ever was.

It is now over 4000 years since God spoke to Abraham (see page 8 for more about this). Since that happened, the Israelites, and later the Jews, have believed that they belonged to a very special religious faith.

Secular Jews

Today many Jews do not practise or follow their faith. They do not celebrate the Jewish festivals, observe **Shabbat** or attend worship in the synagogue. They do not follow the special Jewish laws about food and diet. Such people are called **Secular** Jews. Yet they cannot turn their backs entirely on being Jews. They remain Jewish – and many are very proud to do so.

What does it mean to be a Jew?

For most Jews being Jewish means:

- believing that God created the world and made himself known to a long line of men and women. Their stories are told in the Jewish Scriptures

- keeping the strict food laws and running a home based on those laws. You will find out more about this on page 36

- celebrating such Jewish festivals as **Pesach**, **Rosh Hashanah** and **Shavuot**. We will look at all of these festivals, and others, in Unit 7

- celebrating the different ceremonies and rituals that extend from the birth of a baby to the death of a person. These include **Brit Milah** and **Bar Mitzvah**. You can find out more about these in Unit 6

- sharing in the worship and life of the local synagogue.

Celebrating festivals forms a very important part of Jewish community life. Why do you think that celebrating is so important? What do you think are the most important times in a person's life to celebrate?

Close links

A non-Jewish person (called a **Gentile**) can be converted to the Jewish faith. This happens after a long period of instruction. However, it is very unusual. Jews do not try to convert people to Judaism.

The vast majority of Jews are born into the faith. As a result, a close link exists between the Israelites and Jews of the past and those alive today. This link has led many people to speak of the 'Jewish family'.

As you will discover in this book, the Jewish religion is all about living. Being a Jew in the modern world means following a clear way of life. This way of life, as we will see, is laid down in the Jewish Scriptures.

- What are 'Secular Jews'?
- What does it mean to be a Jew?
- What unites all Jews, living and dead?

For your dictionary

Bar Mitzvah is the ceremony which marks the coming of age of a Jewish boy at the age of 13.
Brit Milah is the Jewish ceremony of circumcision carried out on every eight-day-old Jewish boy.
A **Gentile** is a person who is not a Jew.
Pesach is the Jewish festival of Passover, which celebrates the release of the Jews by Moses from Egyptian slavery. It is also known as Passover.
Rosh Hashanah is the Jewish New Year, the time for remembering God creating the world.
Secular Jews are people who are born Jews, but who do not follow a Jewish way of life.
Shabbat is the seventh day of the week, the Jewish day of rest, also known as the Sabbath Day.
Shavuot is the Jewish festival marking the beginning of the wheat harvest.

1 The Jews in these photographs come from very different backgrounds. They do, however, have a great deal in common. What do you think really binds them together?

> I was born a Jew and I cannot lose that. In fact, I am very proud to be a Jew. You could argue that Jewish people have given more to the modern world than any other group of people. Yet I do not follow most of the traditional Jewish practices.

> My Jewish faith has always meant a great deal to me. I try to live my life according to the Jewish Scriptures. I married a Jewish man and we have tried to bring our children up as God-fearing Jews.

 Look back

Abraham (page 5)
Israelites (page 5)
Jew (page 5)
Judaism (page 5)
Moses (page 5)
Scriptures (page 5)
Synagogue (page 5)

2 These two Jewish people are talking about their Jewish faith and what it means to them today.
a What word can be used to describe the Jewish man?
b What reason does he give for his pride in being a Jew – although he does not follow the Jewish religion?
c How does the Jewish woman express what it means to her to be a Jew?

7

From the past
Who was Abraham?

Abraham is a very important religious figure in the history of both Islam and Christianity, as well as Judaism. We read of his life in **Genesis**, the first book of the Jewish Scriptures

We are not quite sure when Abram, or Abraham as he was later called, lived. He was probably born in the Middle East between 2000 and 1800 BCE.

Abraham meets God

Abraham was brought up in the small town of Ur near the Persian Gulf. Like everyone else there, he worshipped many gods. However, at some time he came to believe in one God. We do not know how or when this happened. But we do know that he taught his family to believe the same as he did.

What is important is that this change in Abraham's and his descendants marks the beginning of the Jewish faith. Abraham came to believe in the God who controlled both the creation of the world and human history. This same God wanted to enter into a **covenant** (an agreement) with Abraham. Under the terms of this agreement:

- God would have a special relationship with the Jewish people. Abraham, and his children, would be the start of a new nation. The story of this relationship, and how it worked out, is told in the Book of Genesis in the Jewish Scriptures.

- God would make special demands on the Jewish people. He would expect them to live differently from all the other people around. Just what those demands were will become clear when you reach pages 10–11.

As a result of meeting with God, Abraham uprooted his large family from Ur. They travelled first to Haran and then on to **Canaan**. This is the country which is known as Israel today.

God had promised Abraham that his descendants would become a great nation. This worried Abraham because he was well into old age and did not have any children. But his wife **Sarah** gave birth to a child when she was much older than the normal age for having a baby. The child was called **Isaac**.

The Patriarchs

The Jewish nation grew out of Abraham's descendants. Abraham, his son and his grandson are called 'patriarchs' (father figures). They are regarded as the founders of Judaism.

- Isaac was Abraham's son. According to the Torah, God commanded Abraham to sacrifice Isaac. Just as Abraham was about to plunge a knife into Isaac, God ordered him to stop. He was really just testing Abraham's faith.

- **Jacob** was Isaac's son. A severe shortage of food in Canaan led Jacob and his family to settle in Egypt. Many years later, a new

Why did Abraham take his family on the journey that you can see on this map? What had happened to Abraham before he undertook the journey?

Egyptian ruler called a **pharaoh** came to the throne. He made Jacob's descendants (the Israelites) his slaves. Their slavery was to last for more than 400 years. You can find out the rest of the story on pages 10–11.

- Who was Abraham?
- What was a covenant and what did the covenant made by God with Abraham demand?
- Who were the Patriarchs?

Look back

Abraham (page 5)
Israel (page 5)
Judaism (page 5)
Scriptures (page 5)

For your dictionary

Canaan was the land promised by God to Abraham and his descendants.
A **covenant** is an agreement made between two parties. Each side has to keep his side of the agreement.
Genesis is the story of 'beginnings'. It is the first book in the Jewish Scriptures.
Isaac was a patriarch and the son of Abraham.
Jacob was a patriarch and the son of Isaac.
A **patriarch** is the name given to a founding father of the Jewish nation.
A **pharoah** was an Egyptian ruler.
Sarah was the wife of Abraham.

1 In the Jewish Scriptures God tells Abraham that he must take his family on a long journey into foreign territory. Read the passage below for yourself and answer the questions that follow.

'The Lord said to Abraham, "Go forth from your native land and from your father's house, to the land that I will show you:
I will make you a great nation and I will bless you.
I will make your name great and you shall be a blessing.
I will bless those that bless you and curse those that curse you:
and all the families of the earth shall bless themselves by you."' (Genesis 12.1–3)

a What does God tell Abraham that he must leave behind?
b How will Abraham know that he has arrived at the destination?
c What promises does God give Abraham for the future?

2 Abraham had to travel almost 1000 miles to reach Canaan. Imagine that you are either Abraham or Sarah. Write a brief diary of the journey, concentrating on some of the problems you would have to face.

What were the Ten Plagues?

Moses, an Israelite and the greatest of the **prophets**, was born in Egypt, where the Israelites had been slaves for over 400 years. When a baby he was found on the banks of the River Nile and was brought up by the daughter of the Egyptian pharoah. He was chosen by God to lead the Jews out of slavery.

Why was Moses forced to leave Egypt?

When Moses was a young man he killed an Egyptian slave-master. He found the man mistreating an Israelite. Fearing for his life, Moses was forced to flee across the Red Sea and into the desert. It was in the desert that God spoke to Moses and told him to return to Egypt. He was God's chosen person to lead the Israelites out of their slavery and into the '**Promised Land**' of Canaan.

The Ten Plagues

Moses did as God told him. He returned to Egypt and demanded that the pharoah set his slaves free. The pharoah refused. To persuade him, God brought ten different plagues down on the Egyptians. Each one was intended to be worse than the one before. They were:

1   The waters of the Nile turned red. They looked like blood.

2   A plague of frogs invaded Egypt.

3   Gnats attacked both people and animals.

4   Swarms of insects covered Egypt.

5   All of the Egyptian livestock (animals), horses and donkeys, camels, cattle and sheep died.

6   People were afflicted with boils.

7   Hail and fire fell down on Egypt from heaven.

8   A plague of locusts covered all Egyptian land. (Locusts eat almost everything in sight.)

9   The land of Egypt was covered by total darkness for three days.

10 The eldest male in every Egyptian household was killed by God. The Jewish festival of Pesach recalls all the plagues and this one in particular.

The plagues persuaded the pharoah to let the slaves, led by Moses, leave Egypt.

The Pesach festival

The last plague gives the name to the most important of all Jewish festivals – Pesach (or Passover). The Angel of Death (God) 'passed over' all the Israelite houses and only killed the eldest sons in the Egyptian houses. All the Israelites had daubed blood on the lintels of their doorposts to show where they lived. Moses had told them to do this.

How do you think the Egyptian parents felt when they discovered that their eldest sons had been killed during the night? Who do you think they blamed for this?

On the first night of Pesach, at a special meal, a drop of wine is spilled for each of the ten plagues. This is to remind everyone of an important truth. It is that although the plagues led to the deliverance of the Israelites from slavery, it also brought great suffering and sadness to the Egyptians. The Israelites were even told off by one of their leaders for singing a happy song together about the way that God had destroyed the Egyptians!

You can read more about Pesach on pages 90–3.

Crossing the Red Sea

After the Israelites had left Egypt, the pharoah changed his mind about letting them go. His army caught up with the Israelites on the shores of the Red Sea. According to the Jewish Scriptures, God parted the waters with a strong wind which allowed the Israelites to pass safely through. The waters then came together again and the whole Egyptian army was drowned. The Israelites were safe to make their way to the Promised Land.

For your dictionary

The **Promised Land** was the land of Canaan. It was promised by God to Abraham and his descendants. A **prophet** is a man or a woman who brings God's message to the people.

Look back

Abraham (page 5)	Moses (page 5)
Canaan (page 9)	Pesach (page 7)
Israelites (page 5)	Pharoah (page 9)
Jew (page 5)	Scriptures (page 5)

- What is Pesach (the Passover)?
- Why is it called the Passover?
- How was the pharoah persuaded to let the Israelites leave Egypt?
- How did the Israelites cross the Red Sea – and what happened to the Egyptians?

1 These drawings show the ten plagues that hit the Egyptians.
a Draw your own version of each of the plagues.
b Write one sentence underneath each one to explain that plague.

2 Copy out this paragraph and fill in the blanks as you go.
_____ was one of _____ most important _____. As a baby he had been found by the _____ _____ on the banks of the _____ _____. As a young man, though, he was forced to leave _____ in a hurry. This was because he killed an _____ _____ who was mistreating a _____ _____.

3 Imagine that you were an Egyptian at the time of the plagues.
a Which of the different plagues do you think would have upset you the most? Explain why.
b What do you think your attitude towards the Israelite slaves might have been after the last plague?

What was the Exodus?

The long time that the Israelites spent in Egyptian slavery has left a lasting impression on the Jewish people. So, too, has their escape from that slavery, which is known as the **Exodus**. After that escape, the Israelites travelled on foot through the wilderness to the Promised Land of Canaan. The journey lasted 40 years. The memory of these events is kept alive in the annual Jewish festival of Pesach.

You can trace the journey that the Israelites took after crossing the Red Sea on the map below. It is quite clear that they did not take the quickest possible route! We do not know why. Perhaps they did not have a clear idea where they were going. They might have been waiting for God to show them the way.

On the journey in the wilderness the Israelites grew in number as other tribes joined them. They may have felt safe from their enemies if they belonged to such a large group. By the time they reached Canaan 40 years later there were probably over 1 million of them in the group.

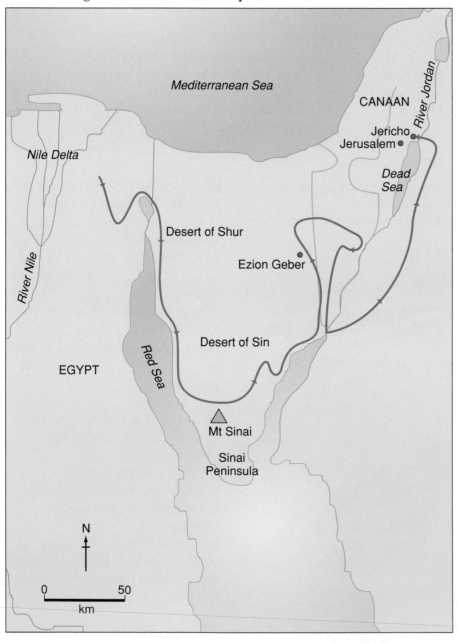

The Ten Sayings

On the journey towards Canaan, the Israelites arrived at the foot of Mount Sinai. Moses left the Israelites and climbed up the mountain to meet with God. God spoke to Moses out of a cloud. In the Jewish Scriptures, God often spoke to people through clouds. This was because humans were too sinful to meet with God face-to-face. Such meetings also often took place on mountains.

While he was in the mountain, God gave Moses many laws for the Israelites to follow. These laws fell into two clear groups:

- laws to cover the everyday lives of the Israelites. They covered such matters as diet, marriage, divorce, punishment and the settling of disputes. There were 613 of these laws.

- the **Ten Sayings**. These are the most well-known laws of all time. The first four cover the Israelites' relationship with God ('You must have no other god before me', 'You must not make a carved image', etc.). The other six cover a person's relationship with other Israelites ('You shall not commit adultery', 'You shall not commit murder', 'You shall not steal', 'You shall not bear false witness', etc.). Together they add up to a very important code of laws.

Moses did not reach the Promised Land himself. According to the Torah, he died when he could see the Promised Land in the distance. He was so close – and yet so far. He had guided the Israelites safely through many trials and tribulations. The actual job of leading them into Canaan fell to **Joshua**. He was to become one of the Jews' greatest leaders.

* What happened on Mount Sinai?
* What were the Ten Sayings?
* How did the Israelites reach the Promised Land and who was leading them at the end of the journey?

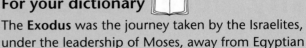

For your dictionary

The **Exodus** was the journey taken by the Israelites, under the leadership of Moses, away from Egyptian slavery into freedom.

Joshua was the Israelite leader who took control on the death of Moses, and led the Israelites into Promised Land of Canaan.

Mount Sinai was the mountain in the desert which Moses climbed to receive the laws, particularly the Ten Sayings, from God.

The **Ten Sayings** are the ten laws which God gave Moses indicating how the people should behave towards God and towards others. They are sometimes called the Ten Commandments.

Look back

Canaan (page 9)   Pesach (page 5)
Israelites (page 5)   Promised Land (page 11)
Jew (page 5)   Scriptures (page 5)
Moses (page 5)   Torah (page 5)

1 You can read the Ten Sayings for yourself by looking up Exodus 20.1–17. These drawings illustrate some of them.

a Produce your own set of drawings to illustrate them. Set each one of them in the present day rather than in the time when the Ten Sayings were given.

b Write two sentences underneath each drawing to explain how that Saying could apply to life in the modern world.

c Make up your own Ten Sayings for people living today. How do they compare with those given by God to Moses?

2 God often spoke directly to people in the Jewish Scriptures. Why do you think:

a He almost always did so out of a cloud?

b The encounter usually took place in a mountain? What was special about a mountain?

Why were the Jews exiled?

Although God had promised them that they would have Canaan as their home, it was not easy for the Israelites to conquer that land. It was a long time before the land was completely in their hands. After the last enemy had been defeated, Canaan was divided amongst the twelve tribes that made up the Israelites.

Even then, from time to time, one tribe or another came under attack from its neighbours. Most of these attacks were easily beaten back. However, the Philistines were a different kind of enemy. They had learned how to smelt iron and build chariots. The Israelites felt very threatened by them. So they asked **Samuel**, a prophet, to choose a king for them, to help them in their fight for survival. He chose **Saul**.

Saul was Israel's first king. He was killed in battle with the Philistines two years after becoming king. He was followed by his son-in-law, **David**, who was Israel's king for 40 years. David was Israel's most loved king. He spent much of his time at war with Israel's enemies, but when he died the country was safe and secure. David's name is attached to many of the **Psalms** in the Scriptures.

David's son, **Solomon**, followed him and built the most beautiful **Temple** in **Jerusalem**. From the

What do you think are the most important things that a group of people lose when their home is taken away from them?

moment that King David had captured Jerusalem, it had become the capital of Israel. Now Jews from all over Israel came to worship God in the Temple in the city three times a year. When Solomon died, however, the kingdom fell apart and the people began to fight each other.

Two separate kingdoms sprang up – Israel and Judah. They did not last long. Israel fell in 721 BCE to the Assyrians and Judah was conquered in 586 BCE by the Babylonians. The Jews were taken into exile (they had to leave Israel). Solomon's Temple in Jerusalem was completely destroyed. The Jewish people had lost their homeland.

For centuries most of the Jews stayed in exile. Those that did return home found that, in 63 BCE, their country was once again conquered. This time it was the Romans who took it over (they called it Palestine). They put Herod the Great on the throne of Israel. Although the Jews hated him, he did rebuild the Temple in Jerusalem. In 66 CE the **Zealots** led a revolt against the Romans. The outcome was disastrous. To punish the Jews, in 70 CE the Romans destroyed Jerusalem and the Temple

This is a model of Solomon's Temple in Jerusalem. Read 1 Kings 5.3–5. Why did King David not build a temple in Jerusalem dedicated to the worship of God?

brick by brick. According to one description:

'*...not one stone was left standing on another.*'

Jerusalem was later rebuilt, but the Temple was never replaced.

For your dictionary

David was Israel's second and most-loved king. He made Jerusalem the capital of the country, and was known as a warrior, poet and leader of the people.
Jerusalem is a city in Israel. It was first conquered by King David and became capital of Israel. It is still very important to Jews, Christians and Muslims.
The **Psalms** are religious songs used in worship in the Temple.
Samuel was the last of the judges in Israel and a prophet.
Saul was Israel's first king. He was killed in battle.
Solomon was David's son and Israel's third king. He built the Temple in Jerusalem. A second Temple was built by Herod the Great.
The **Temple** in Jerusalem was a beautiful building built by Solomon in which to worship God.
The **Zealots** were a group of Jews who were fanatically opposed to the Romans.

Look back

Canaan (page 9)	Promised Land (page 11)
Israel (page 5)	Prophet (page 11)
Jew (page 5)	Scriptures (page 5)

The Roman soldiers destroy Jerusalem. Once again the Jews found themselves in exile. Find out when they were finally able to return to their homeland.

- Why did the people of Israel ask Samuel to find them a king?
- What happened to Israel after the death of King Solomon?
- Why did the Romans destroy the city of Jerusalem brick by brick?

1 These words were written by a Jew who was in exile in Babylon:

'*By the rivers of Babylon*
There we sat and wept
As we thought of Zion.
There on the poplars
We hung up our lyres...'
(Psalm 137.1,2)

a Find another word that means the same as 'exile'.
b What do you think that the people who sat and wept by the waters of Babylon were weeping about?
c 'Zion' was another name for a city in Israel. What do you think that city was called?

d Another word for 'poplar' here is 'willow'. Why do you think we speak today of 'weeping willows'?
You will have to use your imagination to answer one or two of these questions.

2 Why do you think that:
a the Jews decided that they needed a single leader to deal with the menace of the Philistines?
b after the death of Solomon the kingdom fell apart?
c many exiles preferred to stay in Babylon rather than return home?
d the Zealots were able to persuade their fellow-countrymen to rebel against the Romans – even though they could not hope to defeat them?

What is anti-Semitism?

Most of the early followers of Jesus, the carpenter from Nazareth, were Jews. For some time Christianity, the religion which grew out of Jesus' teaching, was an off-shoot of Judaism. Tension soon developed between the old and the new faiths. Clear traces of this tension, called **anti-Semitism**, can be found in the Christian Scriptures – the **New Testament**.

Although the two faiths soon separated, one thing continued to unite them. They both suffered greatly at the hands of the Romans. Then, in 312 CE, the Roman Emperor, Constantine, became a Christian. A new wave of persecution was soon directed against the Jews alone. Many Christians saw this persecution as a suitable punishment for the Jews. This was because their New Testament taught that the Jews had plotted to kill Jesus.

This picture shows Crusaders going off to battle. What do you think was the main reason for the Crusaders attacking the Jews during the Crusades? Clue: Look again at the introduction above.

When William the Conqueror invaded Britain in 1066 he brought many Jews with him. They settled in the largest towns. Before long many of them had become very successful businessmen. They were particularly involved in lending money. Soon many people owed them large sums of money. This led to them being widely hated.

The Jews were persecuted in many English towns – particularly London, York and Norwich. A terrible massacre took place in York in 1190 when some Christians burnt many Jews to death in a tower. In 1290 all Jews were expelled from Britain and not allowed back until 1656. The same thing was happening all over Europe at this time.

During the Crusades, in the eleventh and thirteenth centuries, Christians set out for Palestine (the Holy Land) to fight against the Muslims. Palestine is the land now known as Israel. They wanted to recapture this land for Christianity from the Muslims. In countries along the way, these armies often settled old arguments with the Jews – thousands of Jews were attacked, robbed, raped or burnt alive.

The Christian Church laid two main charges against the Jews. Christians believed that the Jews:

- were responsible for the death of God's Son, Jesus Christ. It was the Jews who persuaded the Romans to crucify him

- murdered Christian children and used their blood in their own religious worship. This rumour first sprang up in Medieval Britain, but soon came to be believed elsewhere.

Anti-Semitism elsewhere

Anti-Semitism soon became widespread in Europe. In his battle with the Roman Catholic Church in the sixteenth century, Martin Luther the Protestant leader sought the help of the Jews. He thought that they would soon convert to Christianity. When they did not, he turned against them. He said that the Jews deserved to have their synagogues burned to the ground.

In Germany during the 1930s the **Nazis** reached similar conclusions, but for different reasons. They blamed the Jews for the German defeat in the First

- What is anti-Semitism?
- Why did the British begin to hate the Jews after the time of William the Conqueror?
- Why has so much hatred been directed against the Jews down the centuries?

Look back

Jew (page 5)
Judaism (page 5)
Synagogue (page 5)

Why do you think that anyone would want to do this to Jewish graves? How do you think that Jews feel when this happens to the graves of those they love?

World War (1914–18). They used that to stir up hatred against the Jews in Germany.

The Nazis believed that Germans were the 'master race' who should control the world. The Jewish people, on the other hand, were more faithful to the traditions of their religion than to the country of Germany. The only solution, the Nazis believed, was to eliminate all Jews. You can find out how they tried to do this on pages 18–19.

Unfortunately, Jewish people are still taunted and, in some instances, persecuted. In recent years, for example, there have been occasions when Nazi signs (swastikas) have been painted on Jewish graves.

For your dictionary

Anti-Semitism is hatred directed against a person simply because they are a Jew.
The **Nazis** were members of a political party which came to power in Germany in the 1930s. Their leader was Adolf Hitler. They were responsible for the deaths of 6 million Jews in Europe during the Second World War.
The **New Testament** is the most important part of the Christian Scriptures. It contains the Gospels and letters written by early Christians.

1 In Nazi Germany in the 1930s, fun was often made of Jewish people in public.
a What is the hatred called that is directed against Jewish people?
b Why do you think that the Nazis set out to make fun of the Jews before they started arresting and persecuting them?
c German children were taught in school to hate Jews. Why do you think that the Nazis wanted young Jews to be hated by their non-Jewish friends?

2 Anti-Semitism still exists today. Spend the next two weeks looking for any examples in the newspapers or on television. Start to talk about many of the important questions raised by anti-Semitism:
a Why are Jews still being picked on in many countries in the world?
b How do people, especially young people, learn to be anti-Semitic?
c Do you think that your own generation is anti-Semitic in any way?
d The Nazis persecuted Jews, gypsies and homosexuals. Are there any groups in Britain that are picked on by others? (To persecute someone means to mistreat them because of their race or religion.)
e Do you have any ideas about how anti-Semitism might be fought, and defeated, in the future?

What was the Holocaust?

No group of people in history has suffered as the Jews did in the Second World War (1939–45). Adolf Hitler and the Nazis tried to wipe them out completely. The destruction of a whole nation of people is called **genocide**.

In just six years over 6 million Jews were put to death. More than 1 million of these were children. They were not a threat to anyone. They lost their lives simply because they were Jews.

What happened in Germany and elsewhere in Europe during this time was horrific. Looking back, Jewish people today speak of those awful years in their history as the **Holocaust**. This word from the Jewish Scriptures means 'a sacrifice'. In some mysterious way those who died were a sacrifice for those who survived.

To begin with Jews were arrested and given the most menial public work to do. Their rights as German citizens were taken away from them. They were forced to wear badges to show that they were Jews. Many of their synagogues were destroyed.

Then, between 1939 and 1945, Jews in Europe were rounded up in vast numbers. They were sent to concentration camps to be eliminated. There were 28 concentration camps altogether in Germany and elsewhere in Europe. Amongst them were those at Dachau, Buchenwald and Belsen. The worst of all the concentration camps, however, was at **Auschwitz**. By 1944, 6000 Jews were being killed in gas chambers every day in this one place alone. Trains brought Jews to the camp from all over Europe.

Yad Vashem

When the Second World War ended people discovered just how many Jews had been killed. The rest of the world was shocked by news reports and photographs from the concentration camps. Few of them had any real idea of what had been going on as news of the concentration camps had been kept secret.

The Jewish community worldwide felt that the world should never be allowed to forget just what had happened. Special prayers were written to be

The Star of David is one of the most frequent symbols of the Jewish religion. This one, in a synagogue in Britain, is a reminder of the Holocaust. Why do you think that it is surrounded by barbed wire?

used in worship. Regular days were set aside to remember the tragedy. Places of remembrance were built.

Yad Vashem, in Jerusalem, is a very special place. The name itself means 'a place and a name'. The 'place' is just a bare room lit by a single candle. The 'names' are those of the different concentration camps inscribed on the floor. There is another special place at Yad Vashem. It is a line of trees – The Avenue of the Righteous. A tree has been planted for every Gentile who helped a Jew during the war. Many Gentiles lost their lives doing this.

- What happened in the concentration camps during the Second World War?
- What is the link between Yad Vashem and the Holocaust?
- What is the Avenue of the Righteous and who is commemorated there?

For your dictionary

Auschwitz was a concentration camp in Poland which opened in 1940. It received 6000 people a day to be killed.

Genocide takes place when an attempt is made to wipe out a whole nation or group of people. The **Holocaust** is the phrase used to describe the Nazi attempt to wipe out the Jewish nation.

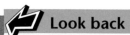

Look back

Gentile (page 5)
Jew (page 5)
Nazis (page 17)
Scriptures (page 5)

1 This photograph shows the Yad Vashem memorial in Israel. Look at it carefully.

a Why is the memorial to the victims of the Holocaust called Yad Vashem?

b What do Jews mean when they refer to the events between 1939 and 1945 as a 'holocaust'?

c Why do you think that this memorial is a particularly suitable reminder of what happened in the Holocaust?

2 One of the worst concentration camps was in Dachau. It is now a museum and this inscription is to be found on one of its walls:

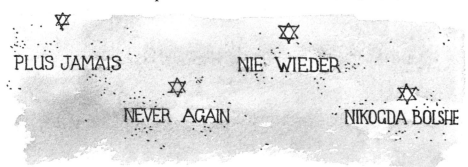

PLUS JAMAIS   NIE WIEDER

NEVER AGAIN   NIKOGDA BOLSHE

a Do you recognise each of these languages? Why do you think the inscription is in these languages?

b Think of two ways in which we could make sure that the Holocaust never happens again.

c Do you think that young people today are aware of what happened in the Holocaust? Should they be?

How did the Jews return to Israel?

The Jews rebelled against the Romans in 66 CE, but their revolt was crushed ruthlessly in 70 CE. The vast majority of them were forced to leave Israel in a hurry. They were soon scattered all over the world – an event which is called the 'Diaspora'. Only a handful of Jews remained in the country of Israel.

Although some Jews drifted back to Israel in the centuries that followed, nearly all of the people who migrated there were Arabs. Most of these were Muslims (followers of Islam). By 1900 only one in ten people living in Israel was a Jew. Conflict between the Muslims and the Jews was bound to take place sooner or later because both religions disliked and distrusted each other. They both believed that God had given them areas next to each other as their homeland.

At the start of the twentieth century, more Jews began to drift back to Israel – or Palestine as it was called. By 1935 the number going back had increased considerably and the Arabs who had lived there for centuries were alarmed. Fighting between the two groups broke out. The British Army which was responsible for policing the area went to the assistance of the Jews. The Arabs were defeated but the problems of the area were only just beginning.

After the Second World War

Millions of Jews died in the Holocaust, but thousands also survived. When the Second World War ended in 1945 they found themselves without a home. They looked upon Palestine (Israel) as their natural home. They thought that they would be allowed to settle there but as they reached the Palestinian coastline they were turned away by the British army. The British were afraid that the new Jewish immigrants would fight with the Arabs. The Arabs did not want any Jewish immigrants at all. The British were under attack from both sides.

The **United Nations** was set up in New York at the end of the Second World War to stop any future world wars. The 'Palestine Question' was almost the first problem it had to deal with. It decided that Palestine should be divided equally between the Arabs and the Jews. The Arabs rejected the arrangement and no agreement was reached.

However, events moved very quickly. The British army left Palestine and the Jews declared the independent State of Israel. The homeland of Israel was again in Jewish hands after a break of 1900 years. Most of the Arabs left the country having lost the land which had been their home for centuries.

Why did the British stop Jewish immigrants from entering Palestine after the end of the Second World War?

- Why was there conflict between the Arabs and the Jews in the early part of the twentieth century?
- How was the State of Israel formed?
- What happened between the birth of the State of Israel and the signing of a peace agreement in 1994?

In 1948 and 1949 a war was fought between the Arabs and the Jews. As a result over 1 million Arabs were left homeless. They had become refugees. Many of them, and their children, still are. Two further wars were fought, in 1967 and 1973, when the Jews took even more land from the Arabs and neighbouring countries. Finally, in 1994, a peace agreement was signed between the Arabs and the Jews. The two groups have agreed to live side by side peaceably, although many differences between them still remain to be settled. Peace in the area is very fragile.

For your dictionary

The **United Nations** is the organisation founded after Second World War to stop any future world war.

Look back

Holocaust (page 19)   Jew (page 5)
Israel (page 5)   Scriptures (page 5)
Jerusalem (page 5)

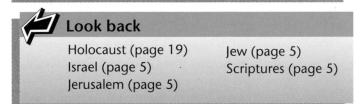

1 The photograph shows the agreement of peace between the Israelis and the Palestinian Arabs in 1994. Find out just what the situation is as you read this. Has the peace been maintained?

2 The prophets writing in the Jewish Scriptures looked forward to a time when the Jews would once again live in their own homeland. Read these two extracts from their writings:

'And I will restore my people Israel;
They shall rebuild ruined cities and inhabit them;
They shall plant vineyards and drink their wine;
They shall till gardens and eat their fruits.
I will plant them upon their soul, never more to be uprooted from the soil I have given them...' (Amos 9.14,15)

'Thus said the Lord of Hosts. There shall yet be old men and old women in the streets of Jerusalem. Each with staff in hands because of their great age...I will save my people from the lands of the east and from the lands of the west; and I will bring them home to dwell in Jerusalem.' (Zechariah 8.3–8)

a What were the Jewish people to do on their return to their homeland?
b What name was to be given to Jerusalem on the people's return?
c What future promises were the people given?

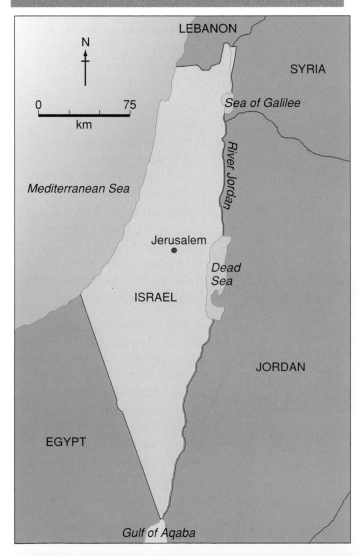

What are Orthodox and Reform Jews?

For a very long time all Jews followed the teachings of the Torah and worshiped in a similar way. The majority of Jews still do. They are called **Orthodox** Jews. These Jews hold very firmly to the teachings of the Torah, or Law, as that was revealed by God to Moses. They insist that its teachings over such issues as the diet and the observance of Shabbat must be kept.

Since the nineteenth century, however, an increasing number of Jews have begun to feel that some of the laws in the Torah were out-of-date. They feel that the Jewish faith needs to be brought up-to-date. They have become known as **Reform** Jews.

The two groups now exist side by side in Britain and in other countries. In Britain today, 9 out of every 10 practising Jews belong to an Orthodox synagogue.

There are three important things to notice about the difference between Orthodox and Reform Jews:

- Their attitude towards the Torah is very different. For Orthodox Jews, the Torah is God's greatest gift to the Jewish people and has been since it was given to Moses on Mount Sinai. It has always been God's Word. It cannot be altered or changed in any way. It does not come in or go out of date. It is always the same. The laws in it must always be obeyed.

  Reform Jews believe that God gave the Torah to Moses centuries ago. At the time it was God's Word to the Israelites. However, things change, and parts of the Torah no longer apply. The Torah must be studied very carefully to see which parts should still be kept.

- The way in which Shabbat is kept is different. On this day Orthodox Jews do not do any work. They do not prepare or cook food, use their own cars or light any fires on Shabbat. Reform Jews do not keep Shabbat as strictly as Orthodox Jews. They prepare food on the holy day, work and use public transport.

- The way that women are treated is different. In an Orthodox synagogue, men and women are separated for worship. Men sit in the well of the synagogue and women in the balcony. Only men are able to read from the Torah in public and only boys have a Bar Mitzvah. Women play no part at all in the public worship.

  In a Reform synagogue, both sexes sit together for worship and women take part in the service. Women are invited to read from the Torah during synagogue services while girls have their **Bat Mitzvah** at the age of 12, which also includes reading from the Torah in public.

These are Hasidic Jews. They are Orthodox Jews. They keep the Torah very strictly. Their clothes and hairstyle come from the eighteenth century when the movement was born. What do you think is the attraction to many Jews of keeping the Torah strictly?

For your dictionary

Bat Mitzvah is the service in a Reform synagogue which recognises that girls become adults at the age of 12. It is equivalent to Bar Mitzvah in an Orthodox synagogue for a boy.

An **Orthodox** Jew is a Jew who believes that the Torah should always be obeyed, and that ways of worshiping do not need to be changed.

A **Reform** Jew is a Jew who believes that some laws in the Torah do not apply any longer, and that ways of worshiping need to be brought up-to-date.

Look back

Bar Mitzvah (page 7)
Israelites (page 5)
Jew (page 5)
Moses (page 5)
Mount Sinai (page 13)
Shabbat (page 7)
Synagogue (page 5)
Torah (page 5)

- What is an Orthodox Jew?
- What is a Reform Jew?
- What is a Bat Mitzvah?

1 This is a photograph of a Reform synagogue.

a Imagine that a service is being conducted in this synagogue on Shabbat. How would you be able to tell that the service was being held in a Reform and not an Orthodox synagogue?

b How might Jews from the two different groups differ in the way that they have prepared and celebrate Shabbat?

c In what way will a Jewish boy and a Jewish girl know whether they are being brought up in an Orthodox or a Reform synagogue?

2 The position of women in reform synagogues is rather different to the way they are treated in Orthodox synagogues. This is one of the most important differences between the two groups and their approaches to worship. Put yourself in the position of a Reform Jew and discuss these two comments:

One of the main reasons why I am a Reform and not an Orthodox Jew is the way that the two traditions treat women. It cannot be right to separate men and women as they take part in synagogue worship. Surely a family, men and women, can pray and sing praises to God together? I think a family gains a great deal by worshipping God together.

My parents grew up in an Orthodox synagogue but when they had three daughters they joined a Reform place of worship. They believed that it was important for girls to grow up to feel part of the synagogue worship just as boys do. I am very glad they did. My Bat Mitzvah was very important to me.

Beliefs
Who is God?

The Jewish Scriptures assume that God exists. They do not set out to prove that He does. All of the Scriptures are a demonstration that He does. The very first verse of the **Tenakh**, the Jewish Bible makes this clear:

'In the beginning God created the heavens and the earth.' (Genesis 1.1)

God was there before the very beginning. Two facts of life place this beyond any argument for Jews:

* the existence of the world that God has made

* the history of the Jews.

The Shema

Every morning and evening in the synagogue and in the home Jewish people say the **Shema**. This prayer is taken from the Scriptures. It declares the most basic of all Jewish beliefs – that there is just one God. There is no limit to God's power. He has created everything in nature and it is all under His control. He has created every form of life, including human beings, and they too are under His control. Nothing is outside God's control.

Nothing happens in this world without God's permission.

The Shekinah

God is therefore over all things. Yet He is not isolated from the world. He does not simply live in heaven. God is close to everything and everyone that He has made. God is here, there and everywhere. Time and time again in the Jewish Scriptures we read of God speaking to human beings – such as Abraham, Moses and David. He was found just where they were. He shared their lives and was sad, upset, happy and loving just as they were.

It is exactly the same today. The Jews have a word to describe this closeness of God. It is called the **Shekinah**. This simply means that God is present everywhere. There is no place in this universe where God is not present. The **Talmud**, the Jewish holy book, tells us that:

'There is no place without the Shekinah.'

So:

* God controls the whole of the universe. He is greater than it. He rules over it. It is under His control.

* God can be experienced in the whole of nature. Every creature and every human being reflects God in some way. The Jewish Scriptures say that human beings are made in the 'image' of God. In a unique way, human beings reflect something of the nature of God.

* God shows Himself in history. Time and time again, in the Jewish Scriptures, God intervenes on behalf of His people. The most important of these occasions are recorded in the Scriptures and re-lived through the festivals which are held each year.

What do you think that Jews mean when they say that all forms of life are under God's control?

- What are the two most important beliefs that Jews hold about God?
- What important point does the Shema make about God?
- What is meant by 'Shekinah'?

שְׁמַע יִשְׂרָאֵל יְדוָֹה אֱלֹדֵינוּ יְדוָֹה אֶחָד וְאָהַבְתָּ אֵת יְדוָֹה אֱלֹדֶיךָ בְּכָל לְבָבְךָ וּבְכָל נַפְשְׁךָ וּבְכָל מְאֹדֶךָ וְהָיוּ הַדְּבָרִים הָאֵלֶּה אֲשֶׁר אָנֹכִי מְצַוְּךָ הַיּוֹם עַל לְבָבֶךָ וְשִׁנַּנְתָּם לְבָנֶיךָ וְדִבַּרְתָּ בָּם בְּשִׁבְתְּךָ בְּבֵיתֶךָ וּבְלֶכְתְּךָ בַדֶּרֶךְ וּבְשָׁכְבְּךָ וּבְקוּמֶךָ וּקְשַׁרְתָּם לְאוֹת עַל יָדֶךָ וְהָיוּ לְטֹטָפֹת בֵּין עֵינֶיךָ וּכְתַבְתָּם עַל מְזֻזוֹת בֵּיתֶךָ וּבִשְׁעָרֶיךָ וְהָיָה אִם שָׁמֹעַ תִּשְׁמְעוּ אֶל מִצְוֹתַי אֲשֶׁר אָנֹכִי

For your dictionary

Shekinah means 'glory'. It is used in Judaism to express the belief that God is present everywhere.

Shema means 'hear'. It is a prayer taken from Deuteronomy 6.4. It is recited by all Jews twice a day.

The **Talmud** is a collection of Jewish laws made between 100 and 500 CE.

The **Tenakh** is the popular name for the Jewish Bible. It is taken from three initial letters for the sections in the Bible – Torah (Law), Nebiim (Prophets) and Ketubim (Writings).

1 The Shema is the most important statement of Jewish belief. It is a quotation from Deuteronomy 6.4–5 and says:

'Hear, O Israel! The Lord is our God, the Lord is one! And you shall love the Lord your God with all your heart and with all your soul and with all your might.'

a Learn the words of the Shema by heart.
b The Shema says one very important thing about God. This statement is at the heart of everything that the Jew believes. What is it?
c Find out on which two occasions the saying of the Shema is important as an act of worship.

2 Jews believe that everything is under the control of God. These drawings show two parts of life which are believed to be under God's control.

a Put two more drawings into your book to show parts of life that are under God's control.
b Explain, in two sentences, what Jews believe about God controlling all things.

3 The Jewish Scriptures say that men and women are made in 'the image of God'. What do you think they mean?

Look back

Jew (page 5)
Scriptures (page 5)
Synagogue (page 5)

What is the Covenant?

When two people make a **covenant** with each other, they enter into an agreement. In any agreement there are duties on both sides. If one or other of the sides fail to keep the agreement then it can break down.

The relationship between God and the Jews is based upon a covenant. The agreement was made between God and Abraham. The special relationship which the Jews have with God is based on this covenant.

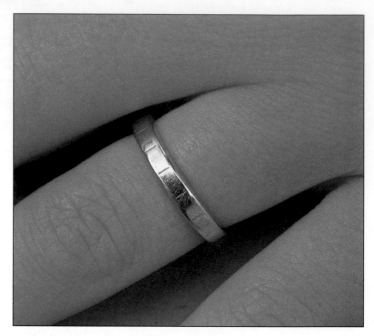

A wedding ring is a universal symbol of an agreement between two people. What do a man and a woman promise each other as they marry?

Jews have always believed that they have a special relationship with God. Some Jews have been happy to call their nation the 'Chosen People' although others have felt uncomfortable with this. However, Jews do believe that their relationship with God is unique.

Making the Covenant

This unique relationship is a covenant in which two groups, God and the Jews, have made certain promises to each other. Should either side break their promises then the other side can end the covenant. The Jewish Scriptures are full of examples of the Jews failing to keep their promises to God. But God never ended His covenant with the people of Israel.

Although the covenant between God and the Jews was first made by Abraham, God only spelt out its terms to Moses on Mount Sinai. It was there that the Jews were given the rules by which they were expected to live. We will look at these rules (**mitzvot**) on page 28.

Both sides of the Covenant

God's side of the Covenant is quite clear. He promised the Jews that He would:

• be their (Israel's) God

• give them a land to call their own.

Although God threatened to abandon His agreement with the Jews on many occasions, He never did so. However the Jews behaved, God always kept His side of the Covenant.

God made demands on the Jews in return. If He was to be their God, they must dedicate themselves to serve Him. God would not allow any rivals. The people could not worship any other gods. The Ten Sayings make this clear:

'You shall have no other gods besides me. You shall not make for yourself a sculptured image...for I, the Lord your God, am an impassioned God.' (Exodus 20.3–5)

This meant that the Jews would always have to be faithful to God. Their nation would be different from all others around because they would follow God's laws. However, there were many occasions when the Jews failed to live up to God's demands. He often punished them but never forgot His agreement with them.

• When Jews speak of having entered into a covenant with God what do they mean?
• What responsibilities did God and the Jews have towards each other because of their covenant?
• What were the Ten Sayings? What did they demand from the Israelites?

 This photograph shows the Ten Sayings which are displayed at the front of most synagogues. They are in Hebrew and just list the beginning of each of the Sayings. Read the Sayings for yourself in Exodus 20.1–17.

If you look carefully you will see that the Sayings can be divided into two groups – a Jew's obligations to God and a Jew's obligations to his or her fellow-Jews. Draw up a table like the one below to illustrate this.

The Ten Sayings

Obligations to God	Obligations to neighbours
1	1
2	2
3	3
4	4
	5
	6

2 Find as many examples as you can of these Sayings being kept or broken today. Look at newspapers, television programmes, etc. Discuss with other members of the class those Sayings which seem to apply to modern life, and those which do not.

What are the mitzvot?

The word **mitzvot** (singular 'mitzvah') means 'commandments'. These commandments are the rules which God has given the Jews to keep. They were given to Moses while he was on Mount Sinai. He then taught them to the Israelites while they were travelling across the wilderness.

The most well-known of the mitzvot are the Ten Sayings. However, there were 613 mitzvot altogether. Of these, 248 told the Jews how they were to live their lives, and 365 mitzvot outlined the things that Jews were not allowed to do.

The mitzvot were intended by God to cover the whole of Jewish life:

- those areas of life which most people would see as religious, for example:
  - The Israelites were told to worship God and no other.
  - They were not to make any kind of statue or image of God.
  - The first-born amongst their children and their animals were dedicated to God.
  - They brought the first-fruits of their harvest to God.
  - They travelled to the Temple in Jerusalem for the three annual 'pilgrimage festivals' – Unleavened Bread, Harvest and Ingathering. These festivals are still kept each year although they are now given different names.
  - They kept the seventh day of the week as one of rest.

  The Jews kept all of these laws because God had told them to do so.

- those areas of life which do not seem to be religious, for example:
  - If an Israelite kept a slave, he was to be set free after six years.
  - The penalty for killing someone else or striking one's own parents was death.
  - No one was to spread false rumours.
  - Witches and those who worshipped any other gods were put to death.

The commandments also covered divorce, the conduct of trials and the food which Israelites were and were not allowed to eat.

Why have the mitzvot?

If you look at the mitzvot carefully you will see that there are clear reasons for keeping many of them. The Israelites lived in the wilderness. There were probably more than 500 000 of them altogether towards the end. Their numbers were growing all the time. Some laws were needed otherwise their lives together would have been impossible.

The reasons for other laws, however, are more difficult to understand. It seems that the purpose of many of the mitzvot was to provide some discipline for the Israelites. Through keeping them, they learned how to treat one another. They also learned that those who hurt others could expect to be punished. To us the punishment is often harsh. At the time, however, it was no harder than that practised by the other tribes.

Some of the mitzvot were intended to test and develop the faith of the Israelites. The **kosher** rules about food, for example, do not appear to have any real purpose – unless it was to teach the Israelites the important lessons of self-discipline and faith.

The Israelites were a nomadic (wandering) community. Spreading false rumours and gossip was severely punished. Can you suggest why?

One of the mitzvot forbade any Jew lending money to a fellow-Jew and charging him extra money (interest) to pay it back. If they lent money to someone they were not allowed to charge interest on it. Would this idea work today? What would be the arguments in favour of it – and against?

For your dictionary

Kosher means 'fitting' or 'correct'. It refers to all categories of food which a Jew is allowed to eat, and also to the preparation of the food within the laws.

Look back

Israelites (page 5)
Jew (page 5)
Mitzvot/mitzvah (page 27)
Moses (page 5)
Ten Sayings (page 13)

• What are mitzvot?
• Why was it important that the Israelites were given many laws and commandments as they walked through the wilderness?
• What was the purpose of the mitzvot?

1 **a** Take any five of the laws mentioned in this unit. You will find them between Exodus 21 and 23. Find out exactly what was outlawed and what the punishment was in each case. Then copy out the laws into your book, together with the punishment. Explain why you think these particular laws were introduced.

b Find five laws which have not been mentioned in the unit. Work out why these laws were passed on to the Israelites. Copy them out into your books with the punishment.

c Imagine that you have been given the responsibility of setting the laws for a large group of people travelling across the desert. Which laws would you introduce? Give reasons for your choices.

2 The Jewish Scriptures say:

'And now, O Israel, what does the Lord your God want of you? To walk in His ways...to keep, for your own good, the commandments of the Lord.'

a Two answers are given to the question at the beginning of this quotation. What are they?

b What reason is given for the keeping of the mitzvot?

What are the Jewish holy books?

The most important book in the Jewish faith is the Tenakh – a popular name for the Jewish Bible. This document is written in Hebrew and is thousands of years old. There are three parts to it:

- The Torah – the books of the Law

- The Prophets, which contains 16 books written by Jewish prophets and many books of history

- The Writings, which includes books of psalms and proverbs as well as two books of history – Ezra and Nehemiah.

The other important Jewish holy book is the Talmud.

The scrolls of the Torah are held up in front of the congregation before it is read. Why do you think this is done?

The Tenakh
The Torah
The books of the Torah (meaning 'teaching') is the part of the Tenakh which Jews value most highly. It covers the first five books of the Bible – Genesis, Exodus, Leviticus, Deuteronomy and Numbers. It is valued so highly by Jews because it tells the story of how God chose them and gave them their laws and land.

The Torah plays an important part in Jewish worship. It is divided into 54 sections and one is read on each Shabbat. The scrolls, called the **Sefer Torah**, are also read on each festival morning. The person reading from the Torah always follows the passage with a **yad**.

The Prophets
The prophets were God's spokesmen. Their writings are amongst the most beautiful in the Tenakh. There are three long books in the Prophets – Isaiah, Jeremiah and Ezekiel – and many shorter ones. Readings from the Prophets accompany those from the Torah in synagogue services.

The Writings
Although these writings are not so important as the Torah and the Prophets

they do contain the psalms. These are used regularly in synagogue worship. Readings from the Writings are usually given on festival days.

The Talmud

For centuries a great number of judgements and opinions passed by Jewish teachers built up. They were all to do with the way that the Jews were expected to behave. These important pieces of information were passed down by word of mouth.

The Tenakh

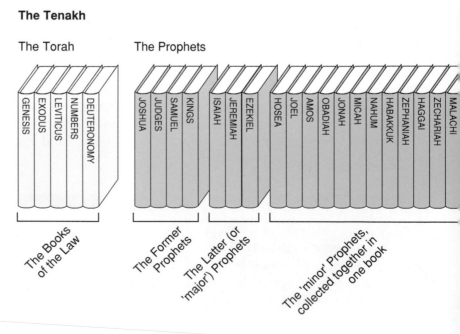

The Torah

GENESIS · EXODUS · LEVITICUS · NUMBERS · DEUTERONOMY

The Books of the Law

The Prophets

JOSHUA · JUDGES · SAMUEL · KINGS

The Former Prophets

ISAIAH · JEREMIAH · EZEKIEL

The Latter (or 'major') Prophets

HOSEA · JOEL · AMOS · OBADIAH · JONAH · MICAH · NAHUM · HABAKKUK · ZEPHANIAH · HAGGAI · ZECHARIAH · MALACHI

The 'minor' Prophets, collected together in one book

This man is reading the Talmud. Which two books were brought together to form the Talmud?

Then, in around 200 CE, they were collected together into one document – the Mishnah.

People then began to discuss the Mishnah. Soon there was more material. This was collected together into the Gemara. The Mishnah and the Gemara were brought together to form the Talmud. This is a very large book indeed. It still has a great effect on the way that Jewish people live. Jewish people sometimes refer to it to try to work out how they should behave in certain situations.

The Writings

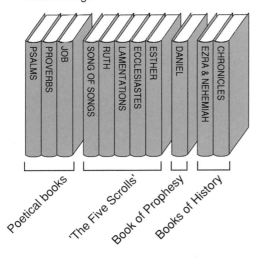

PSALMS
PROVERBS
JOB
SONG OF SONGS
RUTH
LAMENTATIONS
ECCLESIASTES
ESTHER
DANIEL
EZRA & NEHEMIAH
CHRONICLES

Poetical books
'The Five Scrolls'
Book of Prophesy
Books of History

- What is the Torah and what does it contain?
- What is the Prophets?
- What is the Talmud?

For your dictionary

The **Sefer Torah** are the scrolls of the Torah which are kept in the Ark in the synagogue.

Yad means 'hand'. A yad is a pointer in the shape of a hand which is used when reading the Torah scroll in the synagogue to keep the place in the text. This means that a person does not have to touch the sacred text.

Look back

Hebrew (page 5)
Jew (page 5)
Prophet (page 11)
Shabbat (page 7)
Talmud (page 25)
Tenakh (page 25)

1 The reading of the Torah stands at the very centre of public worship in the synagogue.
a How do Jewish people show, in practice, the importance that the Torah has for them?
b What is the difference between Orthodox and Reform synagogues as far as those who are able to read the Torah in public is concerned
c Why do you think that it is looked upon as a great honour to be chosen to read from the Torah in the synagogue?

2 There are several mistakes in this paragraph. Work out what the mistakes are and write the correct version in your book.

The most important part of the Jewish Bible is the Torah. It contains four books – Genesis, Exodus, Psalms and Deuteronomy. It starts off with the creation of the world and ends with the giving of the Ten Sayings on Mount Ararat. The Torah is divided into 52 portions and these are read each day in the mosque but not on Shabbat. Readings from the Writings, such as Isaiah and Jeremiah, are also read alongside the Torah.

Who is the Messiah?

In the Jewish Scriptures the Jews were promised a Messiah. This was to be a man chosen by God who would arrive on earth at the end of time. He would then deliver the Jews from all their enemies and set up the Kingdom of God on earth. Some Jews believe that the setting up of Israel in 1948 brought the coming of Messiah very close. Others are far from sure.

On many occasions in their history the Jewish people have been cruelly persecuted – or taken captive in another country. Whenever this has happened the Jews have prayed to God. They have asked Him to send them a leader who would inspire them to fight against their enemies – a Messiah. This person would have God-given powers of leadership and wisdom. The Jews' enemies would be unable to resist him and they would be free.

The promise

For almost 3000 years Jews have lived with the promise of the coming of the Messiah. The promise is repeated time and time again in the Jewish Scriptures. They make it clear that the Messiah will follow in the footsteps of Israel's much-loved King David. He is expected to:

- be called God's son. He is divine
- bring God's blessings with him
- set up God's kingdom on earth. He will be God's representative on earth
- destroy all the enemies of the Jews
- rule over the world for ever.

The Messiah's rule

We have already seen that the Jews expect their Messiah to deliver them from all their enemies. However, there is more to it than that. They expect the Messiah to:

- banish violence, greed and war from the world for all time. The photograph opposite illustrates this
- set up a government covering the whole world in which truth and justice will be experienced by everyone
- set up a religion which people everywhere will share. This religion will be based on the Jewish belief in one God.

For centuries the Jews dreamed of returning to their homeland in Israel. It finally happened in 1948. Why do you think that many Jews expected their Messiah to come after this happened?

- Who is the Messiah?
- What kind of blessings will the Messiah bring to the Jewish people?
- How will the coming of the Messiah affect the world?

To help people to picture what will happen when the Messiah comes, one of the prophets spoke of a world in which the lion will lie down with the lamb. What message do you think he was trying to put across?

1 This Jewish prophet is writing about the coming of God's Messiah. In this quotation he describes just what he expects the Messiah to be like:

'For a child will be born to us, a son will be given to us;
And the government will rest upon His shoulders;
And His Name will be called Wonderful Counsellor,
Eternal Father, Prince of Peace.
There will be no end to the increase of his government or of peace...' (Isaiah 9.6–7)

a Several names are given here to the Messiah. What are they? Write one sentence about two of them trying to explain what you think they mean.
b What do you think the prophet means when he says that 'there will be no end to the increase of his government or of peace...'?

2 Jeremiah was one of the most important of the Jewish prophets. He said this about the Messiah:

'And he will reign as king and act wisely
And do justice and righteousness in the land.
In his days Judah will be kept safe,
and Israel will live undisturbed.' (Jeremiah 23.5)

a What is the Messiah is expected to do when he comes to earth?
b What differences will the people on earth notice when the Messiah comes?

> **For your dictionary**
> **Messiah** means 'God's Anointed One', the one sent to deliver the Jews from all their enemies and to set up God's kingdom on earth.

> **Look back**
> David (page 15)
> Israel (page 5)
> Jew (page 5)
> Prophet (page 11)
> Scriptures (page 5)

What do Jews believe about life after death?

There is no **creed** as such in the Jewish faith. However, during the twelfth century, a very important Jewish thinker, Moses Maimonides, set out his 'Thirteen Principles'. These are still the closest that the Jewish faith comes to a creed or statement of faith.

Two of the Principles deal with life after death. They say that:

- God will reward the righteous and punish sinners in this world and the world to come.

- The dead will rise to life.

There is very little about life after death in the Jewish Scriptures although they do speak of the **soul** surviving after death. The souls of the dead live on in **Sheol** after death. At the same time the soul is able to retain some contact with those who are still living on earth.

The Jewish Scriptures prefer to concentrate on life on earth rather than talk about the after-life. They teach that people should live God-fearing lives and leave the details of any life after death to God. The ideas of Moses Maimonides came long after the Scriptures had been written. The Talmud supports this approach. It issued a warning against any speculation about what might occur in the life after death. It said that as 'no eye hath seen it' so it is foolish to try and work out what God had in mind for human beings after death.

The coming of the Messiah

Jewish minds were much more taken up with the coming of the Messiah. The Messiah would set up God's kingdom on earth. In this way he would make the earth a better place to live in. Righteous Jews who had died would be brought back to life.

However, some people looked beyond this earth. They believe that God's kingdom here is but a stage on the way to God's kingdom in the world to come. In that kingdom the judgement will take place of non-Jews (Gentiles). They will be divided by God's angels into two distinct groups:

- the sinful who will be judged by God and sent to hell. But hell will not last for ever as in other religions, such as Islam. Hell is the place where the souls of the sinful are cleansed and only lasts for 12 months. The cleansed souls can then enter heaven

- the righteous will be changed so that they can share in God's world to come.

Life is too painful to spend time thinking about life after death. The Jews have suffered a great deal. Yet they have kept their faith in God alive. They are content to leave the details of what happens to them after death to God as well.

For your dictionary

A **creed** is a statement of what a religion believes.
Sheol, in the Jewish Scriptures, is the place of the dead.
The **soul** is the spiritual part of a person, the part that survives death and lives in the after-life.

Look back

Gentile (page 7)
Messiah (page 33)
Scriptures (page 5)
Talmud (page 25)

- What did Moses Maimonides say in his 'Thirteen Principles' about life after death?
- What is the basic teaching of the Jewish Scriptures about life after death?
- What warning does the Talmud give to those who want to speculate about life after death?

A Jewish family enjoying each other's company. What do you think these people are likely to believe about life after death?

1 a Write down five things that Jewish people believe about life after death.

b How would you describe the hope that the Jewish faith gives to those who are approaching the end of their lives?

c Jews seem to be rather vague about the details of life after death. Muslims and Christians say a lot more. Do you think that anyone can really know what is going to happen to them after they die? Would you like to – or not?

2 A Jewish midrash is a teaching from a rabbi. One such midrash says:

'People in this world fulfil commandments and do not know the value of what they have gained. In the world to come they will realise what they have achieved.'

a This midrash suggests that people keep the commandments without knowing why. Can you remember what these commandments are called? Clue: look at page 28.

b Why do you think that people in this world fulfil the commandments but do not know the value of what they have gained?

c What, according to this midrash, is the difference between this life and the world to come?

Family life
What are the Jewish laws about food?

There are strict laws about food and diet in Judaism as there are in many other religions. The food which a Jew is allowed to eat is called kosher. The proper ways of preparing such food is also called kosher. The food which is forbidden to all Jews to eat is non-kosher or **treifah**.

Kashrut is the name given to the different laws which decide whether meat is kosher or not. It is the responsibility of a Jewish mother to make sure that the food laws are kept within her own home.

The basic laws governing kosher food are set out in the Jewish Scriptures in Leviticus 11. These say that kosher food includes:

- fish which have both fins and scales. Cod and herring are allowed but shell fish and eels are not

- meat from animals which both chew the cud and have cloven hooves. This means that meat from sheep, cows and goats is allowed, but any pig product is forbidden

- birds that are bred domestically, like chickens and geese. Meat from birds of prey cannot be eaten.

Eggs and milk can be eaten as long as they are taken from animals which are kosher.

Killing animals

Jews are only allowed to eat kosher animals if they have been killed by **shechita**. This means that they have to have been killed by a certified butcher who follows strict guidelines. Every animal must be killed by passing a very sharp knife across its throat to cut the jugular vein. It is claimed that this is the most painless method of killing an animal.

The Torah orders all animals killed for food to be free from blood. So to begin with the animal is hung up until all the blood has drained out. Then the meat is soaked in salty water before it is cooked.

Separating milk and meat

There is a verse in the Torah which says:

'You must not cook a young goat in its mother's milk.' (Exodus 23.19)

Jewish women who run kosher homes take this to mean that meat and milk products must not be cooked or eaten together. They keep separate sets of kitchen utensils and saucepans so that the two can be prepared, cooked and washed up without coming into contact with each other. After they have eaten meat, Jews wait several hours before eating any milk product.

Kosher foods

Non-kosher foods

Look at these animals carefully. Can you think of any practical reasons why the Jews were able to eat some animals and not others?

In areas with large Jewish communities, you will find special kosher butchers. In areas with small Jewish communities a kosher table is often set up in the synagogue. Why do you think that most Jews believe it to be important to continue the old Jewish food laws?

- What is meant by kosher food?
- What are the basic laws governing kosher food?
- What is shechita?

For your dictionary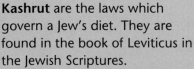

Kashrut are the laws which govern a Jew's diet. They are found in the book of Leviticus in the Jewish Scriptures.
Shechita is the killing of animals by a recognised slaughterer in keeping with the laws about kosher.
Treifah refers to the food which a Jew is not allowed to eat.

Look back

Jew (page 5)
Judaism (page 5)
Kosher (page 29)
Scriptures (page 5)
Synagogue (page 5)
Torah (page 5)

1 Look at the diagram on the opposite page showing the foods that a Jew may and may not eat. Compare the diagram with the list of foods in Deuteronomy 14.3–21.

a Make two columns. In the first list those foods which are kosher and in the second those which are not.

b Imagine that you are inviting a friend round for supper. Your friend follows the kosher rules. Plan a menu keeping within the kosher limits. Compare your menu with that of two other members of your class. Discuss your menus and decide which is the most attractive menu.

2 Look at each of these items. Which of them would be considered kosher and which would not? Explain each of your answers.

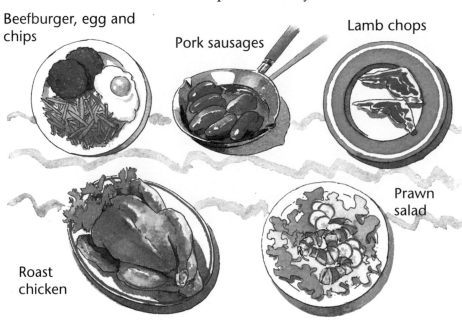

Beefburger, egg and chips

Pork sausages

Lamb chops

Roast chicken

Prawn salad

What is a mezuzah?

For all Jewish families home is a very special place. It is there, rather than in a synagogue, that the most important worship of God takes place. Home is where Jewish parents love and teach their children the traditions of their faith. Home is the place where children learn from their parents just what it means to be Jewish.

Jewish homes have one distinguishing mark which tells outsiders what kind of home it is. This is a **mezuzah** (plural mezuzot). This is a small parchment scroll inscribed with two passages from the Jewish Scriptures. You will find a mezuzah outside every room in a Jewish house except the bathroom and the toilet. There will also be one on the outside of the house itself.

The mezuzah is attached to a doorpost. Why do you think a portion of the Jewish Scriptures is fixed to almost every room in a Jewish house – and to the outside as well?

What is a mezuzah?

A mezuzah is a parchment scroll containing the most important statement of Jewish belief – the Shema. This begins:

'Hear, O Israel! The Lord is our God, the Lord is one!' (Deuteronomy 6.4)

Why put these words on the doorpost of every Jewish home? The Jewish Scriptures have the answer:

'And these words which I command you this day shall be upon your heart...and you shall write them upon the doorposts of your houses and upon your gates.' (Deuteronomy 6.9)

Taking care of a mezuzah

A mezuzah must be handwritten on parchment by a Jewish **scribe**. The parchment (animal skin) which is used must come from a kosher animal. The parchment is then placed within a protective casing before being nailed to the right-hand doorpost towards the top.

Some Jews wet two fingers on their right hand and touch the mezuzah as they go into a room or leave it. This is a sign of the respect that they have for God and for the Torah – from which the words on the parchment are taken.

As a mezuzah is a holy object, care must be taken to keep it in a good state of repair. The writing on the parchment must always be legible. To check this, the case is opened every three years by a scribe. If necessary the parchment is mended or replaced.

Why is a mezuzah important?

A mezuzah is important because of what it symbolises:

- It is a sign of the unity of the Jewish community.

- It expresses the dedication of that community to God.

- It shows that God's Word governs the way that people behave in every part of the house.

- As each person moves around the house and sees the different mezuzot, they are reminded of how much they owe God – and how much He continues to bless them.

Why do some Jewish people touch the mezuzah as they enter or leave a room? What are they trying to show as they do so?

- What stands at the centre of Jewish worship?
- What is a mezuzah?
- Why does a mezuzah have great importance in the Jewish home?

For your dictionary

A **mezuzah** (plural **mezuzot**) is a text from the Bible inscribed on parchment, and hung on the doorposts inside and outside a Jewish house.

A **scribe** is an expert in the study of the Torah and is responsible for producing the scrolls used in the synagogue.

◀ Look back

Jew (page 5) Shema (page 25)
Kosher (page 29) Synagogue (page 5)
Scriptures (page 5) Torah (page 5)

1 Copy out each of these sentences putting the correct beginning with the correct ending.

a A mezuzah is written on	the most important statement of Jewish belief.
b The Shema is	must come from a kosher animal .
c The skin for a mezuzah	near the top of a door post.
d A mezuzah is nailed	parchment made from animal skin.
e By touching a mezuzah	often needs to be replaced.
f The Shema in a mezuzah	Jews are showing their respect for God.

2 This shows what the Shema looks like in Hebrew. Look up the Shema in Deuteronomy 6.4–5 and copy it into your book. Now answer these questions:

a Do Jews believe in many gods or one God?

b How are Jews to behave towards God?

c What are Jews to do to help them to remember the Shema and its importance in their everyday lives?

שְׁמַע יִשְׂרָאֵל יְהוָה אֱלֹהֵינוּ יְהוָה אֶחָד וְאָהַבְתָּ אֵת
יְהוָה אֱלֹהֶיךָ בְּכָל לְבָבְךָ וּבְכָל נַפְשְׁךָ וּבְכָל מְאֹדֶךָ וְהָיוּ
הַדְּבָרִים הָאֵלֶּה אֲשֶׁר אָנֹכִי מְצַוְּךָ הַיּוֹם עַל לְבָבֶךָ וְשִׁנַּנְתָּם
לְבָנֶיךָ וְדִבַּרְתָּ בָּם בְּשִׁבְתְּךָ בְּבֵיתֶךָ וּבְלֶכְתְּךָ בַדֶּרֶךְ
וּבְשָׁכְבְּךָ וּבְקוּמֶךָ וּקְשַׁרְתָּם לְאוֹת עַל יָדֶךָ וְהָיוּ לְטֹטָפֹת
בֵּין עֵינֶיךָ וּכְתַבְתָּם עַל מְזֻזוֹת בֵּיתֶךָ וּבִשְׁעָרֶיךָ
וְהָיָה אִם שָׁמֹעַ תִּשְׁמְעוּ אֶל מִצְוֺתַי אֲשֶׁר אָנֹכִי
מְצַוֶּה אֶתְכֶם הַיּוֹם לְאַהֲבָה אֶת יְהוָה אֱלֹהֵיכֶם וּלְעָבְדוֹ
בְּכָל לְבַבְכֶם וּבְכָל נַפְשְׁכֶם וְנָתַתִּי מְטַר אַרְצְכֶם בְּעִתּוֹ
יוֹרֶה וּמַלְקוֹשׁ וְאָסַפְתָּ דְגָנֶךָ וְתִירֹשְׁךָ וְיִצְהָרֶךָ וְנָתַתִּי
עֵשֶׂב בְּשָׂדְךָ לִבְהֶמְתֶּךָ וְאָכַלְתָּ וְשָׂבָעְתָּ הִשָּׁמְרוּ לָכֶם
פֶּן יִפְתֶּה לְבַבְכֶם וְסַרְתֶּם וַעֲבַדְתֶּם אֱלֹהִים אֲחֵרִים

How do Jews view children?

Children have always been very highly valued within the Jewish community. When they are born they are the most obvious sign of God's blessing on a marriage.

Children are also a sign of hope for the future of the Jewish community. As Jews do not go out of their way to make converts to their faith, the future of Judaism depends on each new generation remaining faithful to its teachings. It brings great sadness when a Jewish person turns his or her back on the faith.

The birth of a baby is greeted with great joy both in a Jewish home and in the wider Jewish community. Jewish tradition insists that the birth of each new baby is the result of co-operation between three people:

- the father
- the mother
- God.

Every child is seen as a gift from God and must be nurtured and loved with the greatest possible care.

Circumcision

There has always been a difference, within Judaism, between the way that young boys and young girls are brought up. This difference is reflected as early as the eighth day of a Jewish boy's life. On that day he is **circumcised**. According to the Jewish Scriptures, God told Abraham, the father of the Jewish nation, to circumcise all the males in his very large family. Ever since then Jewish boys have been circumcised, and always on the eighth day after birth. You will find out more about circumcision (Brit Milah) on page 58.

Naming

Babies are taken to be introduced to the community in the synagogue This is usually the occasion when the child's name is announced. One of the names is taken from the Jewish Scriptures. The congregation take the opportunity to welcome the baby into the Jewish community. It promises to pray for the child and its parents in the years ahead.

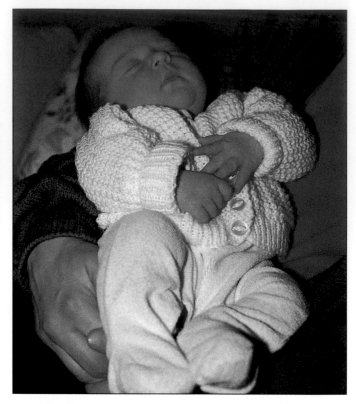

Who has co-operated in the creation and birth of this Jewish baby?

The child's name is announced to the congregation in front of **Ark**. The scrolls of the Torah are kept in the Ark. It is the holiest part of the synagogue. Why do you think the name is announced from here?

Education

Jewish parents want their children to grow up within the faith. This is very important. In its early years, a child learns about Judaism and the traditions of the faith at home. It is a father's responsibility to see that his children study the Torah. Later a child may be sent to a Jewish school but it is more likely, in Britain, that they will go to a non-Jewish school. In this case, a Jewish child will attend special classes in the synagogue to learn how to read and understand Hebrew. He or she will also study the Jewish Scriptures.

- Why are children valued so highly in Jewish communities and homes?
- Who set the example which others follow when they have their male children circumcised?
- What is the part played by parents and school in the education of Jewish children?

For your dictionary

The **Ark** is the cabinet in a synagogue where the Scrolls of the Torah are kept. There was an Ark in Solomon's Temple.

Circumcision is the removal of the foreskin of a boy's penis when he is eight days old. It is also known as Brit Milah.

Look back

Abraham (page 5)
Brit Milah (page 7)
Hebrew (page 5)
Jew (page 5)
Judaism (page 5)
Scriptures (page 5)
Solomon (page 15)
Synagogue (page 5)
Temple (page 15)
Torah (page 5)

1 Answer each of these questions in your own words:

a Why are children so very important to the future of the Jewish faith?

b What do you think people mean when they speak of children as being 'gifts of God'?

c Why do you think that parents announce the name of their child to everyone in the synagogue? Why is it something that interests the community as a whole?

d Why do you think that the Jewish faith, as every other religion, places so much importance on the education of children?

2 Imagine that you are a parent. You have two young children and you are very anxious that they should share your religious beliefs. How would you set about educating them? What would you do? What wouldn't you do?

How involved are Jewish parents in the education of their children?

How are Jews educated?

Education is very important in the Jewish community. As a child grows up so the community takes on more and responsibility for his or her education. Although it was not the case in the past, the education of girls is now given as high a priority as that of boys.

Education does not stop when schooling is over. For Jews it continues through adulthood and into old age. The reason for this is simple. There are 613 commandments (mitzvot) altogether. One of these is to study and learn the Torah. The mitzvot are not withdrawn for a Jew of any age. It is a life-long duty which everyone is expected to carry out.

Education is so very important in the Jewish community because its value is underlined in the Torah:

'The matters which I teach you today you shall take to your heart. You will teach them carefully to your children, and you shall speak of them...' (Deuteronomy 6.6–7)

Jewish schools

There are over 50 000 Jewish children between the ages of 5 and 18 in Britain today. Of this number, about 10 000 go to Jewish schools – from nursery and primary schools through to secondary schools. While these children study the same subjects as children in non-Jewish schools, they also study areas of particular Jewish interest, such as Jewish history and belief. Time is also taken out for the celebration of the Jewish festivals.

After secondary school, most Jewish children go out to work or on to college or university. Boys who want to study Judaism at a deeper level go to **yeshivah.** Some, but by no means all, of these boys go on to be **rabbis** and become responsible for teaching others.

Adult education

In the past most adults set aside some time on Shabbat to study the Torah and the Talmud. Today most synagogues run courses for both men and women. In the more traditional Jewish communities men spend several hours a week studying. They often have a 'companion', another man, with whom they study. This means that they can ask each other questions or try to solve problems between them. They only need to refer to an expert, such as a scribe, when a particularly difficult problem arises.

- What do Jews learn from their holy Scriptures about the importance of studying and education?
- How does the education of some Jewish children differ from that of other children?
- What is yeshivah?

Jewish children dressed for a festival at school. What do you think a Jewish child might gain from being at a Jewish school?

This Russian Jew is studying at the Jewish School in Moscow. Why do you think that Jews try to study their holy books all the way through their adult lives?

For your dictionary

A **rabbi** is a teacher or master. It is the title given to a teacher of Jewish law.

Yeshivah is the place where people sit, the traditional place where men study the Talmud, one of the Jewish holy books.

Look back

Jew (page 5)
Judaism (page 5)
Mitzvah/mitzvot (page 27)
Scribe (page 39)
Shabbat (page 7)
Synagogue (page 5)
Talmud (page 25)
Torah (page 5)

1 Imagine that you are the Jewish parents of children living in an area where there is a large Jewish community. Close to where you live are two schools – one is a Jewish school and the other a popular non-Jewish school.

a How would you expect the education provided by the two schools to be similar – and different?

b What are the advantages, and disadvantages, of sending your child to a Jewish school? Set out your answer in the form of a table.

2 Here are two comments on the importance of learning the Torah from Jewish teachers of long ago.

a *'When two people sit together and words of the Torah pass between them, the presence of God rests between them also.'*

What does this suggest about the high value placed on the Torah?

b *'If as man learns from his fellow a single chapter, a single rule, a single expression or even a single letter, he should treat him with honour.'*

What does this say about the high importance of learning the Torah?

How do Jews view women?

The first two chapters of the Jewish Scriptures, Genesis 1 and 2, seem to present two rather different pictures of men and women:

- In the first, Genesis 1, God created the first man and woman together. They were equal but not the same. They lived together in the Garden of Eden and were equally involved in the first sin – although most of the blame was attached to the woman.

- In the second, Genesis 2, God created man first. The man was given the task of naming the animals in the garden. He returned to God afterwards to report that none of the animals were his equal. God took pity on the man and created the woman to be his 'helpmeet'. The woman was made from the man's rib. The implication was that she was, in some way, his inferior (not his equal).

These two different approaches are reflected in the two very different kinds of Jewish community which exist today.

Women in Orthodox Judaism

In Orthodox Judaism, the traditional attitude towards women, based on Genesis 2, is followed.

- Women do not have to carry out any of the mitzvot. Unlike the men, the women do not say the Shema, wear **tefillin** or take part in the Jewish festivals. Some women choose to do these things but they are not expected to.

- Women do not play any part in public worship. They sit with their young children and older daughters in the gallery of the synagogue while men and sons sit in the well of the building. Jewish girls do not have any real equivalent to the Bar Mitzvah although many synagogues have introduced a ceremony called **Bat Hayil** (Daughter of Valour) for girls on their twelfth birthdays.

- Women have not been expected in the past to learn the Torah, since their domestic and family responsibilities would have prevented this. However, more women are now being given the opportunity to study the Torah and so increase their knowledge of the faith. The importance attached to the education of women and girls has increased considerably.

Women in Reform Judaism

Many Jews belong to Reform synagogues. These are synagogues which do not place such a high degree of importance on the old Jewish traditions. The Torah is important but the old laws do not have to be carried out completely. In these synagogues:

- Jewish girls at the age of 12 have their own ceremony of Bat Mitzvah (Daughter of the Covenant). During this ceremony a girl can read from the Torah – a privilege which, in Orthodox synagogues, is reserved for men.

In this synagogue the men sit in the well while the women and children sit in the gallery. Find out why men and women have traditionally been separated in all Jewish acts of worship.

- Women can train to be rabbis. This involves having a large part to play in the teaching that goes on in the synagogue. Women can also be called up to read from the Torah during public worship.

- There are two different views of women in the Jewish Scriptures. What are they?
- What is the main difference between Orthodox and Reform Judaism in the way that women are treated?
- What is Bat Mitzvah?

For your dictionary

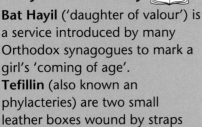

Bat Hayil ('daughter of valour') is a service introduced by many Orthodox synagogues to mark a girl's 'coming of age'.

Tefillin (also known an phylacteries) are two small leather boxes wound by straps around the forehead and arm. They contain four passages from the Jewish Scriptures.

Look back

Bar Mitzvah (page 7)
Bat Mitzvah (page 23)
Genesis (page 9)
Judaism (page 5)
Mitzvah/mitzvot (page 27)
Orthodox (page 23)
Rabbi (page 43)
Reform (page 23)
Scriptures (page 5)
Shema (page 25)
Synagogue (page 5)
Torah (page 5)

1 This photograph shows a woman reading from the Torah scroll in a synagogue service.

a Is this service taking place in an Orthodox or a Reform synagogue? How can you tell?

b What other differences might you notice between the two kinds of synagogue service?

2 There are considerable differences in the role of women in Orthodox and Reform synagogues. Many of these differences are mentioned in the text. Make a table in your book like the one below and complete it.

Men and women in the Jewish faith				
	Orthodox Judaism		Reform Judaism	
	Men	Women	Men	Women
1				
2				
3				
4				

How do Jews view old people?

Like most of the other religions in the world, Judaism places a great emphasis upon the traditions and customs of the past. The past history of the Jewish people is very important. It needs to be preserved and kept alive. It must be handed down from generation to generation.

Older people have a very important part to play in this process. The Jewish Scriptures call these older people 'elders'. Elders have always been the natural leaders in the community. Younger members of the community have always been expected to look up to them and to respect them. This attitude is very much a feature of Jewish family and religious life today.

The Talmud outlines the various stages through which a person passes as he or she grows older:

- At the age of 30 a person reaches their full strength.

- At the age of 40 a person achieves wisdom.

- At the age of 50 a person is fit to advise others.

- At the age of 60 a person enters old age.

- At the age of 70 a person attains grey hair.

Respecting elders

Elderly people bring a great deal of wisdom to their advice. This is why younger people should listen to them. Their wisdom comes from their long and extensive experience of life. The Talmud demanded that great care should be taken of the elderly person who has forgotten his or her learning through senility. Younger people must learn to accept the physical fraility of elderly people.

There is a mitzvah which requires children to honour and fear their parents. Tradition has insisted that this same honour should also be extended to grandparents, although to a lesser extent. In practice this means things like:

- not contradicting their points of view

- not calling them by their first names since this shows a lack of respect for them

- not losing one's temper with them

- standing up when they enter the room

The Jewish faith stresses that elderly people should, if at all possible, be looked after by their family. Why do you think that this is thought to be so important?

- feeding and clothing their parents when they can no longer look after themselves

- speaking respectfully of them after they have died.

If a child can no longer look after his or her parents, he or she must provide for them. A child also has the responsibility of making sure that his or her parents are properly buried and for paying the expenses of their funeral.

- Who carries the main responsibility for looking after elderly people in the Jewish community?
- What is the most important quality which elderly people bring to those around them?
- What responsibilities do Jewish children have towards their parents?

 Look back

Mitzvot/mitzvah (page 27)
Talmud (page 25)

1 Look at this photograph. One of the commandments of Judaism is that people should:

'Rise before a grey-haired person and honour the face of the old.'

a Why do you think that Judaism places such an importance on the respect which is due to elderly people?

b What do you think the commandment means when it says that the young should 'Rise before a grey-haired person'?

c What do you think it means to '...honour the face of the old'? What does it mean to 'honour' those who are old?

2 These two comments are by Jewish young people about older members of their family.

My grandmother seems to bring an immense amount of wisdom to everything that she says and does. It is not easy to explain just what I mean. You know when someone is being wise without necessarily being able to explain what you mean.

Angela, 21

My grandfather is well into his sixties. As a Jew I have been taught to listen to what he says and respect his opinions and wishes. I try to do this but it is not easy. As a young person I have some clear ideas of my own – they do not always agree with my grandfather's opinions. We are taught, however, to act in such a way as not to displease our grandparents.

David, 19

a How do you think it is possible to recognise wisdom in older people? Where do you think that wisdom comes from?

b What do you think it means to 'honour' and 'respect' one's parents and grandparents? Does it always mean doing as they say?

Worship
What is a synagogue?

We do not know when the first synagogue was built. However, we think it happened when the Jews were exiled to Babylon in 586 BCE. The exiles could no longer worship in Solomon's great Temple in Jerusalem. They needed somewhere to worship and praise God.

Even when this Temple was later rebuilt by Herod the Great, the Jews still continued to build synagogues. Later on these buildings were used for far more than just religious worship. They became courts of law and schools as well. They also began to grow into the community centres which modern synagogues have become. They now act as a focus for the whole Jewish community.

Modern synagogues still retain many of the features which the old Temple in Jerusalem had.

To begin with the synagogue was a meeting place for the Jewish community in an area. That is, in fact, just what the word means. Later, however, the building became a place in which Jews studied the Torah and the other holy Scriptures. It has also become a community centre where different groups of Jews meet. Most modern Jews prefer to call the synagogue building by its Hebrew name of **shul**.

This photograph shows the inside of a synagogue. Why is the building so important to Jews today?

Inside a synagogue

All synagogues are built facing the city of Jerusalem, where Solomon built his Temple. The city of Jerusalem is always close to the heart of every Jew.

Step inside a traditional synagogue and you will notice:

- separate areas for men and women. The men pray on the lower floor while the women and girls climb up into the gallery

- the Ark, the most important feature in a synagogue. The Ark is a cupboard at the front of the synagogue which houses the scrolls on which the books of the Torah are written. These scrolls are the holiest objects in the synagogue. When they are not being used, a curtain stretches across in front of them. The scrolls are 'dressed' in special covers with tassels at the end.

- a raised platform which stands in the centre of the synagogue. This is the **bimah**. During a service the Torah is taken to the bimah to be read. As the bimah is a raised platform so the person reading must 'go up' to the Torah. This shows that God's Word, the Torah, is higher than any human being.

Three symbols in the synagogue are also very important. They are:

- the **Everlasting Light** which always burns above the Ark. This light, which burns oil, is never allowed to go out. It symbolises the Jewish belief that God is always present with them in their place of worship and elsewhere.

- two stone tablets on the wall above the Ark in most synagogues. On these tablets the Ten Sayings are written – or at least the beginning of each one. These sayings are at the very heart of the Torah and so underline the importance of the Tenakh.

- the six-pointed **Star of David**, which is made of two equilateral triangles. One of them pointing downwards and the other upwards. This was an ancient symbol of fire and water. In the Middle Ages, it was regarded as a shield against evil.

Why is the Ark a particularly important part of the synagogue?

For your dictionary

The **bimah** is the platform at the front of the synagogue from which the Torah is read.

The **Everlasting Light** is the light which always burns in front of the Ark. It symbolises God's constant presence with His people.

Shul is the Hebrew word for synagogue.

The **Star of David** is a six-pointed star. It is one of the most important symbols of Judaism, and is the national symbol of Israel.

Look back

- What is the bimah?
- What does the word 'synagogue' mean?
- What is kept in the Ark and why are these particularly important?

1 Here are three pictures of symbols found in almost every synagogue:

a Write two sentences about each of these symbols in your book.

b Why do you think that symbols such as these are so very important in religious worship?

2 Hilda is in her late sixties and has been going to her local shul for over 40 years. She finds that it has become more important to her as she has got older.

As children we were always taken to shul by our parents. They were very strict Orthodox Jews. When I grew up there was a time when it didn't seem to matter if I went or not. Then my husband died and the people in the shul were so very kind. Now my social life revolves around it. I enjoy the services and especially those held at festival times.

How would you sum up Hilda's reasons for going to shul?

What happens in a synagogue?

Like all other religious buildings, synagogues come in many shapes and sizes. Some of them are modern, while others were built centuries ago. Some have stained glass windows, while others have plain ones. Some are large and some are small. Wherever a synagogue is found, it offers a refuge of worship, prayer and teaching for every Jew. It also plays other, very important, roles within the Jewish community.

In the past Jewish synagogues have been used for many different purposes. They often had guest rooms to welcome Jewish travellers and their animals. Jewish courts (called **Bet Din**) often met in the synagogue buildings. They still do in some synagogues. The Bet Din is a court of three rabbis which has the authority to rule on matters of Jewish law.

The synagogue also contained a **mikveh** (a bath). People who had been converted to the Jewish faith were immersed in the bath as part of the process of joining the faith. Jewish women also had to wash in the bath after they had their monthly period and after they had given birth to a baby. Strict conditions were attached to the water that was put in the mikveh. The modern synagogue is rarely used for these purposes.

However, many activities still take place in most synagogue buildings. These 'community centres' bring Jews together to:

- celebrate. Synagogues are well used by Jewish people in the area. The most important events in a Jewish person's life – circumcision, Bar Mitzvah and Bat Mitzvah, marriage and death – are all times when people come together. Services in the synagogue are often followed by a celebration. Meetings and lectures are also held in the hall.

- learn. As we saw on page 42, Judaism stresses the importance of learning from the earliest years through to late in life. These lessons usually take place in the synagogue. Children and young people are often taught by the rabbi, and others, on Sunday mornings.

- relax. Youth clubs, creches and mother and baby clubs, clubs for older people, lunch clubs and many other activites all use synagogue premises. This has always been the case. The synagogue has never simply been a place of worship. It has always been a real 'community centre'.

- worship. Every Shabbat Jewish men, women and children come to the synagogue to worship God. They also attend special services for all the Jewish festivals. Although worship mainly revolves around the home for every Jewish family, the synagogue also plays a very important part in Jewish worship.

The Jewish community has always emphasised the importance of celebrating together. Why do you think this is important? Which occasions draw them together in this way?

This Jewish family is eating a Shabbat meal together. How important is the family in Jewish religious life?

- By which name do most Jews refer to the synagogue?
- What do Jews mean when they refer to their synagogue as a 'community centre'?
- What is the relationship between the home and the synagogue as the central place for Jewish worship?

For your dictionary

Bet Din means 'the house of judgement'. It is the name of the court which decides on disputes between Jewish people.

A **mikveh** is a bath that traditionally has been used by Jews for cleansing purposes.

Look back

Bar Mitzvah (page 7)   Judaism (page 5)
Bat Mitzvah (page 23)   Shabbat (page 7)
Circumcision (page 41)   Synagogue (page 5)

1 Imagine that you are a Jewish person living in an area where there are many other Jews. You join a synagogue which has just opened. You find yourself on a committee which has to make the synagogue as widely known in the area as possible.

a Design an advertisement to go into the *Jewish Chronicle* advertising the synagogue.

b Design a leaflet to be put through the doors of Jewish people in the area telling them about the many activities which take place in the synagogue.

2 The scrolls of the Torah are the holiest objects in any synagogue. Carry out some research to discover:

a How these scrolls are made and what material is used.

b What is written on the scrolls.

c What the 'etz chaim' is.

d Who writes and prepares the scrolls.

e Where the scrolls are kept in the synagogue.

f How a new scroll is presented to a synagogue and the celebration that surrounds its reception.

How do Jews pray? (1)

Praying is the most important part of Jewish worship. Jews believe that they can pray to God at any time and in any place. They can do this when they are on their own. However, most Jewish prayer is said in the company of others. This is why certain times are set aside for prayer in the synagogue.

There is one basic rule about Orthodox Jews coming together to pray in the synagogue. They must form a **minyan**. To make prayer a public activity there must be a minimum of ten Jewish males present. This rule has been abolished in Reform and Progressive synagogues.

Jewish men come together to pray. Why do you think that prayer is such an important part of Jewish worship?

Daily prayers

Jewish synagogues hold three services each day:

* morning prayer – Abraham prayed early in the morning so that he could meet with God before the business of the day

* afternoon prayer – Isaac stopped what he was doing to pray to God in the afternoon

* evening prayer – Jacob prayed to God in the evening to thank God for his blessings during the day.

By praying three times a day, Jews are following the pattern set by their forefathers – Abraham, Isaac and Jacob.

The Siddur

The **Siddur** is the Jewish prayer book. In the Siddur prayers have been brought together from many times and places. Some of the prayers are very old going back to around 450 BCE. Others date from this century. Most of the prayers in the Siddur are in Hebrew. A translation of each prayer into the language of the people runs alongside.

The services in the synagogue include many prayers from the Siddur. They also include the most important prayer of all – the Shema. Three other prayers are also included in all of the services:

* the **Amidah** – eighteen blessings (benedictions) which are at the heart of Jewish worship

* the **Aleynu** – a prayer which praises God and prays for Israel and the whole world

* the **Kaddish** – a prayer for holiness which is often used when people are mourning someone who has died.

* Why do Jews pray three times a day, and how do they follow the examples set by their forefathers in doing this?
* What is a minyan?
* What is the Siddur and what is it used for?

1 The Talmud gives this advice about prayer:

'When you pray, do not regard your prayers as a fixed task, but as a plea for mercy and an entreaty before God.'

There are three aspects to this advice which are worth thinking about:

a What does it mean when it says that no one should regard praying as a 'fixed duty'?

b Explain what the words 'plea' and 'mercy' mean.

c What does it mean when it says that all prayer should be an 'entreaty' before God?

2 Here are two comments made by young Jews about prayer.

I live a very busy life. I do not always find time in a day to pray. When I do, however, I always find that it helps me with my life. I normally use the old Jewish prayers. Somehow, it helps if other people before me have prayed the same prayers.

a Why do you think it helps this young Jew to feel that she is using words which others have used before her?

As far back as I can remember my parents always prayed with me and my sister. At the time it was a real nuisance – especially when we were teenagers. Looking back, though, I am glad that I picked up the habit of praying. It matters to me now and I do not think that I would pray if I hadn't been taught to as a child.

b Why do you think that many Jewish parents pray with their children?

How do Jews pray? (2)

Jewish women are expected to pray but they are released from the obligations (duties) relating to prayer. This is because their family responsibilities make set times for prayer difficult. On the other hand, men do have an obligation to pray at certain set times during the day – whether at home, in the synagogue or elsewhere. Although there are no set rules about it, tradition says a man should wear certain clothes and objects as he prays.

The kippah

It is an almost universal custom that all Jewish men cover their heads when they pray. Any headgear is acceptable. However, many wear the **kippah** (also known as the yarmulka) which is a skull cap. Wearing the kippah is a sign of respect. Religious people have always believed that a man should cover his head as he enters into the presence of God.

What is this man wearing on his head? Why do Jewish men always cover their heads when they are praying?

The tallit

After his Bar Mitzvah, a Jewish man is given a **tallit**. This four-cornered shawl is usually made from wool with black or purple stripes across it. At each corner there is a eight-stringed fringe, with a fringe of silver or gold at the top of the shawl. These instructions are carefully laid down in the Torah. The Jewish man today is obeying the Torah, God's Word, whenever he wears his tallit.

Jewish men wear their tallit whenever and wherever they pray during the morning – whether at home or in the synagogue. They also wear it to the synagogue each Shabbat. In some synagogues, however, this does not happen until after the man has married.

Tefillin

Tefillin (also known as **phylacteries)** are very holy objects to all Jewish men. Every male over the age of 13 must wear them while saying his morning prayers – except on Shabbat and festival days. Boys usually start wearing them a week or two before their Bar Mitzvah to get used to them.

Tefillin are two black leather boxes which have leather thongs attached to them. They are worn in exactly the same place by every Jew:

A Jewish man is proudly wearing his tallit. He hopes that he will be buried in the garment. Can you think of one reason why?

* One is wound around the upper left arm in line with the heart.

Why are tefillin worn around the left arm and in the middle of the forehead?

- The other is wound around the forehead so that the box ends up in the middle of the forehead.

This shows that the Word of God must enter the heart and the mind.

Four passages from the Jewish Scriptures are written on parchment inside each box. Two of these passages are the first two paragraphs of the Shema. The other two are from Exodus 13.1–10 and Exodus 13.11–16.

Wearing the tefillin is a response to and a reminder of the commandment of God in the Scriptures 'to bind the word of God between your eyes and upon your arm'. The tefillin are not worn on Shabbat since on that day, unlike the other days of the week, all of the time is devoted to the service of God.

Every three years the tefillin are opened up and checked. If the writing has faded or disappeared altogether, it has to be repaired or replaced. This is done by a qualified scribe.

- How would you describe a kippah?
- What is a tallit?
- What are tefillin?

For your dictionary

A **kippah** is a black skull cap worn by Orthodox Jews when in the synagogue and elsewhere. It is also known as a yarmulka.
Phylacteries is another name for tefillin.
A **tallit** is a Jewish prayer shawl. It is worn by men when praying, and is made of white material with fringes.

Look back

Bar Mitzvah (page 7)   Synagogue (page 5)
Scribe (page 39)   Tefillin (page 45)
Shabbat (page 7)   Torah (page 5)
Shema (page 25)

1 Read Exodus 13.1–10 and 13.11–16. Together with the Shema these two passages are included in every tefillah (singular of tefillin). Now answer the following questions.
a Which day are all of the Israelites told to remember?
b During the seven days of the Pesach festival all Israelites are told to eat one food in particular. What is it? Carry out some research to discover why Jews are told to eat this during Pesach.
c Who brought the Israelites out of slavery in Egypt? What did he have to do to bring this about?
d What other name for tefillin is found in this passage? Why are the tefillin to be worn?

2

a Copy this drawing into your book.
b Draw arrows to the tallit, kippah and tefillin, and name them.
c Explain underneath the drawing the spiritual significance of each of these objects.

Who works in a synagogue?

The Jewish faith relies on many people to meet the needs of everyone in the community. Each of these people has a particular job of work to do. Without their service, the worship life of the Jewish community would be very difficult – if not impossible. Only one of them, however, is full-time and that is the rabbi.

The most important of the workers employed by most Jewish synagogues are:

- the rabbi
- the **chazan**
- the scribe
- the **mohel**
- the **shochet.**

The rabbi

The work of the rabbi in a synagogue is not like that of a priest in a Christian church. The rabbi does not go between God and the worshipper. In Judaism each person is responsible for his or her own spiritual welfare. The rabbi is a person who is highly trained in all aspects of the Jewish faith. He is expected to play several roles in the Jewish community:

- to take part in Shabbat worship, to lead the prayers, read from the Torah and give a sermon. Such worship can go ahead without a rabbi although most synagogue services are led by one

- to carry out weddings and funerals, visit those who are mourning the death of someone, to prepare a couple for their coming wedding. Each of these functions can be performed by someone else if necessary

- to educate members of the congregation in the traditions of their faith. This is the most important role that a rabbi plays as his name means 'teacher'. The continuing education of all ages is very highly valued by the Jewish community

- to visit the sick and elderly

- to form, with two other rabbis, a Bet Din. This 'court of Jewish law' deals with matters which Jewish people prefer to settle within the community. For example, it plays an important part in the granting of divorce to Jewish couples

- to represent and speak up for the Jewish community outside the synagogue. For example, some rabbis work as chaplains in colleges, universities, hospitals and prisons.

The chazan

The chazan (or cantor) leads the singing in some of the largest synagogues. The playing of musical instruments on Shabbat is classified as 'work' and so is not allowed. The chazan chants the prayers in services on Shabbat and festivals – as well as leading the singing at weddings and funerals. Smaller synagogues may not have a chazan.

What is the role of the rabbi in the modern world? Why do you think that he or she is a very important member of the Jewish community?

The scribe

The scribe has a very important job to do. He copies out the new Torah scrolls which are then presented to synagogues. These scrolls are the holiest objects in the synagogue. He also copies the small parchments which are placed within the tefillin and mezuzah.

The mohel

By tradition a Jewish father was expected to circumcise all of his sons. Today, in almost all Jewish communities this delicate task is now carried out by a mohel (circumciser).

The shochet

The shochet is a Jew who is specially trained to slaughter animals according to the laws laid down in the Jewish Scriptures.

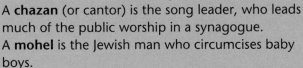

- What work does a scribe do within the Jewish community?
- Why does the Jewish community need to have a chazan to lead the singing on Shabbat in the synagogue?
- Who are the mohel and the shochet?

Why is the work of the scribe considered to be a very important one in the Jewish community?

For your dictionary

A **chazan** (or cantor) is the song leader, who leads much of the public worship in a synagogue.
A **mohel** is the Jewish man who circumcises baby boys.
A **shochet** is the man in the Jewish community who has authority to kill animals in keeping with the Jewish laws.

1 Try to explain what this saying from the Talmud means:

'One should not live in a town that has no scribe.'

2 The best people to tell you about the work they do in the Jewish community are the people themselves.

a Try to invite one of the people who plays an important part in the Jewish community into your school. Find out just what it is that they do. Ask them why their work is considered to be important within the Jewish community.

or

b Arrange a class visit to a local synagogue. Arrange to interview the 'workers' in the synagogue.

From birth to death
What is Brit Milah?

According to an old Jewish saying:

'The whole world rejoices when a baby is born.'

This just about sums up the Jewish attitude when a new baby enters the world. Everyone believes that the baby is a gift from God and so is anxious to welcome him or her into the Jewish family. If the baby is a boy then Brit Milah (circumcision) is part of that welcome.

All Jewish boys are circumcised. In a tradition going all the way back to Abraham, this always takes place on the eighth day after the baby boy's birth. The service is known as Brit Milah.

According to the book of Genesis, God and Abraham had a conversation. God told Abraham to circumcise all the males in his family. It appears to have been a common activity in many old religions. However, for the Jews it became something very special. Two things are important about this:

- It makes circumcision the oldest Jewish tradition of all. No other tradition, still carried out, can be traced back directly to Abraham.

- Circumcision was the sign to all Jews of the covenant that God had made with Abraham. This agreement is the basis of all that Jews believe about God – and themselves.

The circumcision takes place in the baby boy's own home. Tradition does not permit the mother to be present. The child is usually carried into the gathering by his grandmother. The boy is first handed to his grandfather (called the 'sandek') who then hands him on to his father.

His grandfather then takes him back and holds him while the mohel carries out the circumcision. A stroke of a sharp knife removes the foreskin from the baby's penis. The skin is then secured so that it cannot grow back again.

The boy's father then says this blessing over his son:

'Praised be Thou, O Lord our God, ruling spirit of the universe, who has commanded us to enter into the covenant of our father, Abraham.'

The baby is given his name and a drop of wine is placed on his lips. The father drinks the remainder of the wine. The family then celebrates a very happy occasion.

The importance of circumcision

Circumcision does not make a person a Jew. Having a Jewish mother does that. Instead circumcision bestows on the child two important blessings:

- The blessing that the child receives from his father has been very important since the time of Abraham. On the night of each Shabbat, for example, a Jewish father blesses his wife and all his family. It was Abraham who began this custom.

- The baby is welcomed into the Jewish community – and so shares in the blessings of God's agreement with the Jews. Belonging to the Jewish community will bring him many blessings in the future.

- What was the importance of circumcision to Abraham?
- How is circumcision carried out, and who does it?
- Why is circumcision important for every Jewish boy today?

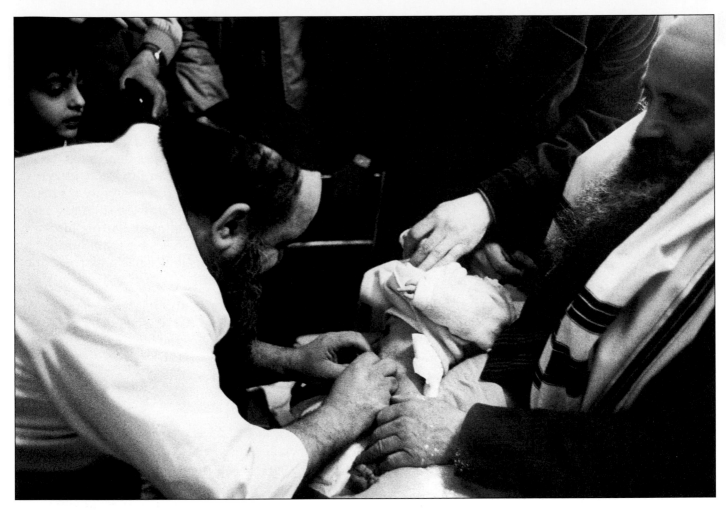

Why do you think that circumcision was originally an act always carried out by the child's father? Why do you think that was important?

Look back

Abraham (page 5)
Brit Milah (page 7)
Circumcision (page 41)
Covenant (page 9)
Jew (page 5)
Mohel (page 57)
Scriptures (page 5)
Shabbat (page 7)
Torah (page 5)

1 In the Jewish Scriptures we read this:

'God said further to Abraham...every male among you shall be circumcised. And you shall be circumcised in the flesh of your foreskin; and it shall be a sign of the covenant between Me and you.' (Genesis 17.9–11)

a Who introduced circumcision for all Jews?
b Who was first told to circumcise all his family?
c Of what does circumcision permanently remind all Jews?

2 After the father has given his blessing to his child, the people respond with these words:

'As he entered into the covenant, so may he enter into a love of the Torah, into the marriage canopy and into the life of good deeds.'

a When and how has the child entered into the covenant?
b What is the Torah which the child must love?
c When will he enter into the 'marriage canopy'?

What is Bar Mitzvah?

At what age do you think a person becomes an adult? In the Jewish faith there are two answers to this question:

- A girl is recognised by the Jewish community as an adult when she reaches her twelfth birthday.

- A boy has to wait a year longer before the Jewish community accepts that he has become an adult.

When a boy reaches his thirteenth birthday, he is considered old enough to take personal responsibility for living out the commandments of the Torah in his own life. Until now his father has taken on the responsibility for his son's spiritual welfare. But from now on he carries that responsibility for himself.

From a very early age each Jewish boy is taught about the history of his religion, his religious faith and the Hebrew language. He is taught both at home by his father and in the synagogue by the rabbi. Some boys go to special Jewish schools, but the majority have to fit in these special studies after school and at weekends. Even at this early age, Jewish children learn that the study of the Torah is one of the most important tasks in life.

By the time a Jewish boy celebrates his Bar Mitzvah ('Son of the Commandment'), on the first Shabbat after his thirteenth birthday, he should be able to read Hebrew. For some time he has been reading parts of the Jewish Scriptures in Hebrew at home. Reading them in public in the synagogue for the first time is an important part of the Bar Mitzvah celebrations.

The ceremony

His Bar Mitzvah is a great and important day in the life of every Jewish boy. There are several parts to the celebrations:

- A 'calling up' to the front during the synagogue service. It is always a great honour for a Jewish man to take part in a synagogue service. A boy is given this honour on his Bar Mitzvah. He can be invited to read from the Torah in public for the first time, to recite a

Jewish blessing or to lead the prayers. He 'goes up' to the bimah to play his part in the service.

- The father's blessing. During the Bar Mitzvah service the boy's father gives thanks to God that his son has reached adulthood. Until now the father has accepted responsibility for his son's spiritual welfare. Now the son must take that responsibility on himself. During his prayer the father expresses his thankfulness to God that this responsibility has now passed from him.

- A gathering. Friends and relations come together for a boy's Bar Mitzvah. During the party after the service the boy makes a short

Relations and friends are in the congregation as this boy celebrates his Bar Mitzvah. Why do you think it is such an important family occasion?

speech. He thanks his parents and teachers for their influence on him. He tells everyone that he hopes to follow faithfully in the ways of his forefathers and the Jewish community to which he belongs.

From this time onwards a boy will wear two important objects which show that he is accepted as an adult male member of the Jewish community. They are his tefillin and tallit.

- What is distinctive about the education and upbringing of a Jewish boy?
- What change takes place for all Jewish boys when they pass their thirteenth birthday?
- What are the main parts of the Bar Mitzvah celebrations?

 Look back

Bar Mitzvah (page 7)   Synagogue (page 5)
Bimah (page 49)   Tallit (page 55)
Hebrew (page 5)   Tefillin (page 45)
Shabbat (page 7)   Torah (page 5)

1 a Why this boy is reading from the Torah in a synagogue service?
  b What preparation has been necessary before this boy can read the Torah in public?
  c Why do you think this is the greatest day in the life of this boy so far? Do you know of any equivalent day in the lives of children who belong to other religions?

2 The father's blessing at the Bar Mitzvah of his son includes the words:

'Blessed is the One who has freed me from the responsibility for this child's conduct.'

a What do you think the word 'blessed' means?
b Who is the 'One' referred to here?
c What has the father been responsible for?
d Who takes over the responsibility from now onwards?

3 a Describe, in a paragraph, a day which was very special in your life. What was it that made it so special?
  b Write a paragraph trying to describe how excited a Jewish boy might be as his Bar Mitzvah draws near. What do you think he is looking forward to most of all? What changes do you think he might notice in his life from this time onwards?

What are Bat Mitzvah and Bat Hayil?

Until this century Jewish women and girls did not play any part in public worship. Their twelfth birthdays came and went without any special recognition in the synagogue. Then Reform synagogues introduced Bat Mitzvah ('Daughter of the Commandment'). Many Orthodox synagogues also introduced Bat Hayil ('Daughter of Valour').

Bat Mitzvah

Reform and Liberal synagogues first introduced Bat Mitzvah in 1923. In these synagogues men and women are treated exactly the same. A girl is recognised as reaching adulthood in a service on Shabbat. Two features in particular are the same as for Bar Mitzvah:

Find out two ways in which males and females are treated differently in Orthodox synagogues?

- A time of education and preparation leads up to this very important and exciting occasion. The girl learns Hebrew so that she can read in public from the Torah scroll.

- There is a party of celebration after the service.

There is one other interesting parallel. Just as the boy's father plays an important part in his Bar Mitzvah, so the girl's mother and grandmother are usually prominent at her Bat Mitzvah.

Bat Hayil

Some Orthodox synagogues now celebrate a girl's coming-of-age. The idea for Bat Hayil ('Daughter of Valour') comes from some words in Proverbs 31.10–31. These describe a 'woman of valour' who is the perfect wife and mother. The words are sung to the woman of the house at the start of every Shabbat by her husband and children. You will find extracts from this hymn below.

The Bat Hayil does not have to be held in a synagogue. The girl does not read from the Torah. The reading of poetry and the singing of hymns play an important part in the service. Everything then ends, as with Bar Mitzvah and Bat Mitzvah, with a party to which friends and relations are invited.

 Look back

Bar Mitzvah (page 7)
Bat Hayil (page 45)
Bat Mitzvah (page 23)
Hebrew (page 5)
Orthodox (page 23)
Reform (page 23)
Synagogue (page 5)
Torah (page 5)

- What is Bat Mitzvah?
- What is Bat Hayil?
- What are the differences between Bat Mitzvah and Bat Hayil?

Why is it still unusual to see a girl reading from the Torah in the synagogue?

1 According to the writer of the book of Proverbs, this is how a good wife can be described:

'Her husband puts his confidence in her and lacks no good thing. She is good to him and never bad...She is like a merchant fleet bringing her food from afar. She rises while it is still night and supplies provisions for her household...She girds herself with strength and performs her tasks with vigour...her lamp never goes out at night...She makes covers for herself...Her mouth is full of wisdom, her tongue with kindly teaching. Her husband praises her...Grace is deceptive, beauty is illusory. It is for her fear of the Lord that a woman is to be praised.' (Proverbs 31.10–31)

a Make your own list of phrases from this extract which describe the woman of virtue using a table like the one below.

The woman of virtue
1
2
3
4
5

b Put a tick by any of these virtues that you think are particularly important today.
c Why do you think that a Jewish girl of 12 is described as a 'daughter of valour'?

2 Deciding when a person is grown up enough to make decisions for themselves is never easy.
a Are you and your parents likely to disagree over when you will be 'grown up'? When do you think it will be? When do they think it will be? Do you think the Jewish faith has it right?
b Why do you think the Jewish faith distinguishes between boys and girls when it comes to being grown up?
c What do you think are the advantages and disadvantages to having an 'official' age at which you are considered to be grown up?

How do Jews view marriage?

The Talmud says that a man is incomplete without a wife. It advises every Jewish man to study first and then to take a wife. However, if he finds it impossible to live without a wife he can reverse the order!

In the Jewish community, weddings are very happy events. Marriage is a gift from God which will bring untold blessings to the couple. They are setting up a new home together and will bring a new generation of Jewish children into the world. They will make a very real contribution to the future of the Jewish faith.

It has always been very important for Jewish people to marry. There is very strong pressure on Jews to marry other Jews. Jews who marry Gentiles cannot have a Jewish wedding in a synagogue. Such a marriage is not encouraged because it can easily run into difficulties. The couple are likely to disagree, for example, over the religious upbringing of their children. It is better for a Jewish person to marry someone who thinks and feels the same way as they do about God.

The Jewish wedding service

Jewish weddings do not have to take place in synagogues – although they usually do. They can be held on any day of the week except Shabbat and festival days. Although a Jewish wedding is much like any other, it does have some distinctive features:

- a period of **fasting**. Before the wedding the bride and groom set time aside to fast. This is important. It allows the couple to seek God's forgiveness for any past sins. They can then start their married life together with a clean conscience

- a special canopy called a **huppah**. The wedding service takes place under this canopy. It is held up by four poles – one at each corner. It represents the home that the couple will build together

- the reading of a **ketubah** (marriage contract). This contract pledges the husband to provide for his wife in case he dies or wishes to divorce her

- the seven blessings. During the service the groom gives his wife a ring. The rabbi then pronounces seven blessings on the couple. These blessings thank God for creating the world and giving such joy and happiness to the couple.

- the breaking of a wine glass. As the service draws to a close the man breaks a wine glass beneath his foot. This reminds everyone that the old Temple in Jerusalem was destroyed by the Romans centuries ago. It also tells the couple that they will have some difficult times ahead in their marriage as well as many good times.

The service in the synagogue draws to a close with everyone in the synagogue shouting out 'Mazel Tov' (Good Luck).

What is the canopy over this Jewish couple called and why is it there?

For your dictionary

Fasting is the practice of going without food and drink to dedicate oneself to God and prayer.

A **huppah** is the traditional canopy under which Jewish couples marry, symbolising the home that they will set up together.

A **ketubah** is the marriage agreement given to a Jewish bride by the groom. It sets out the duties which the groom will carry out on the bride's behalf.

Look back

Gentile (page 7)
Jerusalem (page 15)
Jew (page 5)
Rabbi (page 43)
Shabbat (page 7)
Synagogue (page 5)
Talmud (page 25)
Temple (page 15)

Reading the ketubah under the huppah at the wedding service.

- Why do you think that Jewish wedding services cannot take place on Shabbat or festival days?
- Why do a Jewish bride and groom fast before their wedding service?
- What is distinctive about a Jewish wedding service?

1 a Have you been to a wedding recently? If so, describe what happened. What building was it held in? Which parts of the service stand out in your mind? Can you think of any symbols which played a part in the service?

b Describe three symbols which play an important part in the Jewish wedding service.

c Imagine that you are invited to a Jewish wedding. Which parts of the service do you think you would find most interesting? Would you have any questions to ask when the service was over?

2 Most religions stress the need for people to marry within the faith.

a Do you think that it is easier or more difficult to be married to someone who believes the same things as you?

b Will this be a factor when you choose someone to marry?

c Can you think of three advantages, and one disadvantage, of being married to someone from the same religion as yourself?

d Why is it important from the point of view of the religion for its members to marry others from the same faith?

How do Jews view divorce?

The Jewish faith values marriage very highly indeed. If a marriage is beginning to fail every effort is made to save it. Much of this effort comes from the Bet Din court. This acts as a kind of divorce counselling service as well as the agency which works out the arrangements of the final divorce settlement. It is only when all other efforts have failed that divorce is accepted as inevitable.

The document of divorce

In the Jewish Scriptures (Deuteronomy 24.1–4) the advice to a man wanting a divorce from his wife is that he should get a 'letter of divorce' (a **get**). There was no way for a woman to divorce her husband nor did she have to consent to the divorce. However, steps were taken to protect the woman who was being divorced. This was done through the ketubah – the marriage document which assured a woman that she would be looked after if her husband ever wanted a divorce.

This is a get certificate. Why do you think a woman needs to produce this certificate if she wishes to remarry?

The modern get contains all the details about the husband and wife. It states the exact details of the divorce. The woman must produce the get if she ever wishes to remarry. This is intended to give some real protection to the wife. At the same time there is a real measure of inequality about the Jewish divorce laws. The system does not treat men and women on the same basis.

Until very recently a man could divorce his wife but not give her a get certificate. This meant that she could not remarry if she wanted to. The Jewish community now put pressure on any men who will not give their wives the certificate. They are even threatened with expulsion from their synagogue.

Obtaining a divorce

The proceedure by which a Jewish couple divorce is very simple:

1   The two people must agree that they wish to divorce.

2   They must both attend a meeting of the Bet Din. If this proves impossible then they can send a representative.

3   A scribe writes out the get. The husband then hands the get to his wife in front of two witnesses.

4   The couple are divorced from the moment that the get is handed over.

A woman can ask the Bet Din for a divorce. She can claim that her husband has been unfaithful, treats her cruelly or is unable to father children. The Bet Din may find in her favour. However, it cannot compel the husband to agree to a divorce.

If both agree to a divorce then they become divorced in the eyes of the Jewish community. In Britain, however, they must have gone through the ordinary divorce courts first (a civil divorce). The law demands this. It is only in Israel that such a civil divorce is not necessary.

There is one important difference between a religious and a civil divorce. In a divorce court a couple need to produce a reason for divorcing – **adultery**, separation, etc. The Bet Din court does not require any reason. It is enough that the couple have tried to save their marriage and have failed.

What is the Bet Din court?

For your dictionary 📖

Adultery is a sexual relationship between two people who are, at the time, married to someone else.
A **get** is the letter of divorce which permits a man to leave his wife.

 Look back

Bet Din (page 51)   Scriptures (page 5)
Israel (page 5)   Synagogue (page 5)
Ketubah (page 65)   Talmud (page 25)
Scribe (page 39)

- What was a 'letter of divorce'?
- What is a 'get'?
- How does a Jewish couple obtain a divorce from the Bet Din – and how is this different from the divorce in the courts?

1 This saying about divorce comes from the Talmud:

'Whoever divorces his first wife, even the altar sheds tears on her behalf.'

a This saying from the Talmud is making a very important point. Try to explain what it is.
b Is it surprising that the Jewish faith, which lays such an emphasis on family life, should make divorce so easy? There is a reason for this. Work out what it is.

2 Many people find it very surprising that, in the past, Jewish men but not Jewish women could obtain a divorce.
a Do you think that this is surprising?
b Do you think that it was enough to try and protect the woman from hardship?

3 Imagine that you are a Jewish man or woman. You wish to divorce your husband or wife. Describe, in your own words, the steps that you will have to take to make this possible.

What are the Jewish customs for death and burial?

Within the Jewish community there is a group of people called the **Chevra Kadisha** (The Holy Society) who look after people as their life draws to a close. The responsibility of this group is to carry out the last acts of kindness and make the necessary arrangements for burial. Every member of the Chevra Kadisha is a volunteer.

Every Jew hopes that he or she can spend the last few minutes of their life reciting the Shema. They also say a prayer. There are three parts to this prayer:

- a statement of their belief in the one God who controls everything – including their life

- a plea for help from God in recovering from their illness – if that is possible

- a confession of their sins and a desire to make good all their sins and misdeeds.

They say this prayer as they are surrounded by members of their own family. Each relative in the room makes a small tear in an item of clothing as the person dies. This is to show that they are grief-stricken. People in biblical times used to tear their clothes in two as a sign of their anguish and grief.

Once a Jewish person has died:

- Their eyes and mouth are closed by a close relative. The body is then washed and wrapped in a single linen shroud. A Jewish man may be wrapped in his own tallit. The body is placed in a simple wooden coffin. In death all people are treated exactly the same. This is no time for a display of wealth.

- Burial follows death as quickly as possible. In practice burial is likely to take place within 24 hours.

- A memorial candle is lit. In strictly Orthodox homes, all of the mirrors in the house are also covered.

The burial service itself is brief. During the service, held at the graveside, psalms from the Jewish Scriptures are sung. The Kaddish prayer, the prayer of mourning, is also said. It includes the words:

'Let the glory of God be extolled, let His great name be exalted in the world whose creation He willed. May His kingdom prevail, in our own day, in our own lives, and the life of all Israel. Let us say, Amen...May the source of peace send peace to all who mourn and comfort all those who are bereaved. Amen'

Working together, the mourners then begin to fill the grave with earth. They do this to confirm in their own mind that the person is indeed dead. They are also showing their oneness with the close relatives who are mourning the death.

What does each Jewish person try to do as death approaches? Why do you think that Jews think it is important for a dying person to be surrounded by all his or her relatives?

- What is the Chevra Kadisha?
- Why do you think that those who look after a body after death belong to the 'holy society'?
- How does the Jewish community stress its belief that in death all people are equal?

1 This photograph shows mourners at a Jewish funeral throwing earth into the grave.
a Why do you think that all of the mourners at a Jewish funeral are expected to throw earth into the grave?
b Think of three ways in which a Jewish funeral is different from that in another religion that you know about.
c Jewish people always bury their dead. They do not cremate them. Why do you think this is?

2 This is the last prayer which every Jew hopes to have the strength to pray:

'My God and the God of my fathers, accept this prayer; do not ignore my supplication [request]. *Forgive me all the sins I have committed in my lifetime and may it be your will to heal me. Yet, if you have decreed that I should die...may my death atone for all my sins and transgressions which I have committed before you...Grant me a share in the life to come...'*
(Siddur)

a Who do you think are the 'fathers' being referred to here?
b Who is it who decides just when each believer should die?
c Two things are prayed for in the future. What are they?
d What do you think it means when the dying person asks that his or death should 'atone' for all the sins they have committed?

How do Jews mourn?

Obviously people feel desperately sad when someone close to them has died. Some religions leave people to mourn in their own way. Other religions encourage people to mourn in a particular way. Judaism is one of these religions.

Within Judaism there are strong traditions about the way that a person should mourn and the length of time they should spend doing so. The customs are intended to help people to mourn before gradually returning to normal life.

In Jewish families the next of kin are expected to mourn a person's death. The extent of the mourning depends on the closeness of the relationship. The strictest rules of mourning are for those who have lost a parent or a child.

The Jewish faith stresses that each person dies in the good hands of God. At the same time it lays a particularly strong emphasis upon the need for all involved to mourn. It sets out four stages through which the mourner should pass:

1   From the moment of death until the time when the person is buried. This is only a short time of a day or two. During this time the mourner is called an **onan**. The main task in this time is to arrange for the funeral. The Chevra Kadisha take over all the practical arrangements.

Why do you think that many mourners want to have a headstone in place over the grave as soon as possible?

Onans are released from all other religious responsibilities during this time. They must not eat meat or drink wine. Between the moments of death and burial it is Jewish tradition that someone, either a relative or a member of the Chevra Kadisha, will always stay with the body.

2   A week of mourning follows the funeral. This is the most important time for mourning and is called **shiva**. The mourners stay in their own homes. Three times a day relatives and members of the synagogue visit the homes of the mourners to pray. However, there is no mourning on Shabbat and the mourners attend the synagogue service.

During this week of mourning, the mourners sit on the floor or low stools to receive visitors. They do not cut their hair or nails, shave or wear leather shoes. No music is played. A candle burns in the house night and day.

3   A further period of 23 days then follows, called **shloshim**. During this time the mourners are no longer expected to sit on low stools. People gradually return to work and life returns to normal. By the end of this time many people set up a headstone over the grave. Others leave this until a year has passed since the person's death.

Why do you think that the onan sits on the floor or a low stool to receive visitors?

4 A period of light mourning lasts until the end of the 11th month after the person's death. For the whole of this time the mourners do not listen to any music. The male members of the family say the Kaddish prayer each day. Then, on the anniversary of the death, a candle is kept burning for 24 hours. This is lit by the nearest relative each year for as long as he or she lives.

- What is an onan?
- What is shiva and how does life change for the mourner in the 23 days following the end of shiva?
- How do Jewish people celebrate the anniversary of a person's death?

For your dictionary

An **onan** is a person in the first stage of mourning.
Shiva is the first week of intense mourning.
Shloshim means 'thirty'. It is the first month of mourning.

Look back

What do you think is the importance of a candle being lit on the anniversary of a person's death?

 1 Draw up your own chart showing the customs associated with mourning in the Jewish community. It might look like this:

Mourning		
Time	Name	Customs
		1
		2
		3

2 Explain, in no more than three sentences, the differences between onan, shiva and shloshim.

3 There are two interesting questions in this unit which are worth talking about in class:
a Why do you think that no mourning is allowed on Shabbat?
b Why do you think that all of the practical arrangements for the burial of a person are taken over by the Chevra Kadisha? What does this leave those close relatives who would normally make these arrangements free to do instead?

What is the Jewish year?

The Jewish year is full of celebrations. There are three types of celebration:

- days on which special prayers are said in the synagogue

- festivals which include special services but which allow the working life of the Jewish community to continue as normal

- festivals for which everything stops to allow the Jews to spend much time in prayer.

The important Jewish festivals can be divided into two main groups:

- festivals which look back to important events in Jewish history

- festivals celebrating God's activity in the world and in creation.

Festivals linked to events in Jewish history

These festivals are often associated with miracles, such as Pesach and **Hanukkah**. They celebrate times when God intervened to do something amazing for the Jews. Although these events took place long ago, they have become an essential part of Jewish worship in every age. This is particularly true of the Pesach festival which looks back to the delivery of the Israelites from Egypt. Jews believe that God sent the ten plagues to the Egyptians to force them to let their Israelite slaves go. You will find out much more about the important festival of Pesach on pages 90–3.

The festival of Hanukkah commemorates a much later event in Jewish history. It looks back to the victory of a small army of Jews against overwhelming odds some 2200 years ago. We will return to this festival on pages 86–7.

Festivals celebrating God's activity in the world and creation

Shabbat is the only festival which is celebrated weekly rather than once a year. Each time that a Jew comes to the synagogue on Shabbat, he is remembering that God rested on the seventh day after spending six days creating the world. Jewish people do the same after six days of work. Sukkoth, the harvest festival, is a reminder of God's goodness in His creation.

One festival has no link with either an event in Jewish history or the cycle of nature. This is **Yom Kippur** (the **Day of Atonement**). On this day Jewish men and women look back over the previous twelve months and take stock. They seek God's forgiveness for all the sins they have committed and look for forgiveness from everyone they have wronged and hurt.

> **For your dictionary**
>
> The **Day of Atonement** is another name for Yom Kippur.
> **Hanukkah** is the Feast of Dedication. It celebrates the victory of Jews over the Greeks in 165 BCE.
> **Yom Kippur** is a day for fasting. It ends the time of repentance begun ten days earlier with the festival of Rosh Hashanah.

These people are celebrating the festival of Hanukkah. Find out ten pieces of information about this festival.

- What do most Jewish festivals celebrate?
- Which is the greatest Jewish festival of all and what does it celebrate?
- What is remembered on Yom Kippur?

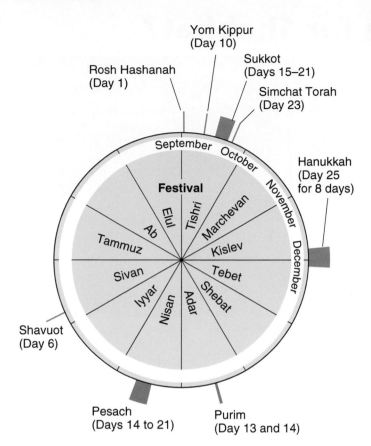

Yom Kippur
(Day 10)

Rosh Hashanah
(Day 1)

Sukkot
(Days 15–21)

Simchat Torah
(Day 23)

September · October · November · December

Festival

Elul · Tishri · Marchevan

Ab · Kislev

Tammuz

Sivan · Tebet

Iyyar · Nisan · Adar · Shebat

Hanukkah
(Day 25
for 8 days)

Shavuot
(Day 6)

Pesach
(Days 14 to 21)

Purim
(Day 13 and 14)

3 Jewish people probably celebrate more festivals in a year than any other group of people. These two comments underline their importance.

> Our religion is the only one which has a weekly festival. Shabbat is a festival for us. On this one day a week we leave work behind to concentrate on prayer and worship. The day is a mixture of the serious and the leisurely. Actually this combination is a feature of almost every Jewish festival.

Samuel

1 Look at the chart before answering these questions:

a Which Jewish festival takes place each week rather than once a year?

b What is another name for the festival of Pesach?

c Which festival is held between 6 and 9 May?

d Which Jewish festival is closest in date to the Christian festival of Christmas?

e When do Jews celebrate their New Year?

f Which Jewish festival lasts for a week and falls during the month of March?

g Two festivals last for a single day and are held in September. What are these festivals?

2 Find out:

a when Shabbat starts and finishes each week. What does this tell you about the Jewish clock?

b how Jews cope with the variations in the seasons as far as celebrating Shabbat is concerned.

> To me the different festivals throughout the year are a very important part of my faith. Some of them, such as Rosh Hashanah and Yom Kippur, are very serious affairs. We spend most of our time seeking God's forgiveness. At others, though, the emphasis is upon celebration and enjoyment.

Isobel

Discuss these two quotations amongst yourselves.

a Why do you think that festivals play such an important part in Jewish life?

b Many of the festivals look back to important events in Jewish history. Why do you think that Jewish people today feel the need to look back to the past?

Look back

Fasting (page 65)	Rosh Hashanah (page 7)
Jew (page 5)	Shabbat (page 7)
Pesach (page 7)	Synagogue (page 5)

How do Jews prepare for Shabbat?

Each week Jews have a day of rest. This is Shabbat, the seventh day of the week. It starts at sunset on the Friday evening and finishes 25 hours later. Shabbat is a time of celebration which looks back to two very important events in Jewish history:

- the creation of the world. God rested from his work on the seventh day after He had spent six days creating the world. We are told that God looked at everything He had created and decided that it was 'good'. Only then did He rest. Jews rest on this day on the principle that what was good for God must be good for His creation, of which they are a part as well.

- the delivery of the Israelites from over 400 years of slavery in Egypt. In the long journey of 40 years through the desert which followed, God gave the Israelites their laws. One of them was to set aside a day of rest each week. This acts as a reminder to all Jews that God will look after them.

Jewish families relaxing together on Shabbat. Why do you think this time is very important?

The word 'shabbat' means 'ceasing'. The custom of ceasing from work, and resting on one day of the week, is a very old one. It marked the Israelites out as being different from all the other nations at that time who expected their slaves and servants to work without stopping. The Israelites stopped work completely on this one day.

The preparations

In every Jewish home Shabbat is different from the other days of the week.

- As no work of any kind can be done on Shabbat, all the necessary work has to be done beforehand. The house must be thoroughly cleaned. All of the shopping has to be done and the food has to be prepared before Shabbat begins.

- The Shabbat table must be laid. The most important part of Shabbat is the meal that the whole family shares together on the Friday evening. Even members of the family who have left home try to return for this meal. New cutlery is brought out. The candlesticks are cleaned and wine is placed on the table. Wine plays an essential part in the meal.

- Each member of the family has a bath and wears their best clothes. They often dress in white to symbolise purity and hope. Candles are often lit before Shabbat begins to drive away sorrow and unhappiness.

The Shabbat preparations involve everyone in the family from the youngest upwards. Although there are synagogue services to attend, the main focus of Shabbat revolves around the home. It is a day for the family to share together.

Look back

Israelites (page 5)
Jew (page 5)
Shabbat (page 7)
Synagogue (page 5)

- What does the word 'shabbat' mean?
- What preparations are necessary in a home before Shabbat begins?
- Why do you think it is important that all of the family is involved in preparing the house for the start of Shabbat?

 1 The table is laid and ready for the start of Shabbat.

a When will this table have been laid?

b When is the special Shabbat family meal held and how important is it considered to be?

c Why do you think that new, or different, cutlery and crockery is brought out for this meal?

d Is there any other occasion when a meal is used to begin an important religious occasion?

2 Here are two comments about the importance of Shabbat. Read them through carefully and think about them.

'[Shabbat helps each Jew] *to achieve rest from the abundance of one's toil so that one might acquire a little knowledge and pray a little more, so that people might meet one another and discuss matters of Torah...*' (a tenth-century rabbi)

a Five reasons are given here for Shabbat being a very important part of Jewish worship. What are they?

'*God said to Moses, "I have a precious gift in My treasure house. 'Sabbath' is its name. Go and tell the people of Israel that I wish to give it to them."*' (The Talmud)

b Why do you think that Jewish people look upon God's gift of Shabbat as one of His most precious gifts?

How do Jews celebrate Shabbat?

Like an old and trusted friend, Shabbat has to be welcomed into the home. Just before dusk falls the mother ushers in Shabbat. She lights the candles and beckons with her hands to welcome in the holy day. She then covers her eyes as she says a blessing and a prayer for her family. Shabbat has begun.

A visit to the synagogue

The males in the family attend an evening service in the synagogue. The females sometimes go as well. In this service Shabbat is welcomed as if it is a bride greeting her husband. The 'husband' is the Jewish people. As the service ends the rabbi takes a glass of wine and recites the prayer of holiness. In this he thanks God for his great gift of Shabbat to the Jewish people.

At home

Before the Shabbat meal begins at home, the family drink wine (the symbol of joy) together. The father then blesses his wife and children. Ever since the time of Abraham the father's blessing has always been very important. He recites the prayer of holiness with each member of the family saying 'Amen' at the end of each blessing.

The Shabbat meal then begins. A special loaf of bread (**challah**) is broken, dipped in salt and eaten. Then, as the meal is eaten, the family sing special songs between the various courses. Stories from the Bible are told to the children. The meal ends with a special prayer of thanksgiving.

The Shabbat service

All of the family attend synagogue on Saturday morning. In Orthodox synagogues the males and females sit separately. In the service which follows:

- The Torah is read. The Torah scrolls are kept in the Ark and when this is opened everyone stands up. The scroll to be read, the Sefer Torah, is taken out and carried to the bimah. The portion can be read by any male member of the congregation. During one year the whole of the Torah must be read in public in 54 instalments.

- After the Torah has been read the rabbi gives his sermon. This will usually be based on the portion that has been read.

- As the people leave the synagogue they wish each other 'Shabbat Shalom' (the peace of the Shabbat).

Havdalah

The final act of Shabbat, **Havdalah** (separation), takes place in both synagogue and home. The ceremony is the same. Wine is drunk, a special candle with several wicks is lit and a spice box is opened to wish every one a happy week ahead. The parting greeting is 'Shavua Tov' as the wine is poured over the candle to put it out.

In this photograph a Jewish girl is welcoming in Shabbat by lighting a candle. Why do you think that the Jewish holy day is welcomed into the home like an old friend?

What is the scroll called which is taken out of the Ark to be read?

For your dictionary

Challah is bread which is specially baked and plaited for use on Shabbat.

Havdalah is the service which brings Shabbat to a close.

Look back

Abraham (page 5)
Ark (page 41)
Bimah (page 49)
Orthodox (page 23)
Rabbi (page 43)
Sefer Torah (page 31)
Shabbat (page 7)
Synagogue (page 5)
Torah (page 5)

- How is Shabbat welcomed into a Jewish home?
- What is distinctive about the service held in the synagogue on Shabbat morning?
- What is Havdalah?

1 Read each of the following quotations carefully:

'For in six days the Lord made the heavens and the earth, the sea and all that is in them, and rested on the seventh day; therefore the Lord blessed the sabbath day and made it holy.' (Exodus 20.11)

a Why did God bless the Sabbath Day and make it holy?

'The sabbath day is a sabbath of the Lord your God...and you shall remember that you were a slave in the land of Egypt...' (Order of Service for the Sabbath Day)

b What are Jews to remember every time they celebrate the Sabbath Day?

'Blessed are you, O Lord our God, ruler of the universe who makes us holy through doing his commandments and has commanded us to light Shabbat candles.' (Prayer said by mother as Shabbat candles are lit)

c What has God commanded His people to do?

2 a The word 'Havdalah' means 'separation'. What do you think is being separated by this ceremony at the very end of Shabbat?

b Why do you think that a spice box is opened at the end of Shabbat – and at the start of a new week?

What is Rosh Hashanah?

Everyone does things they are ashamed of. Sometimes people carry the guilt of their actions with them. The Jews believe that something must be done about sinful actions. To begin with a person must repent of their sins. They must then seeks God's forgiveness. If they have wronged another person, they must try to put the matter right. They can then ask that person for their forgiveness.

The festival when all this takes place is Rosh Hashanah – which marks the beginning of the Jewish New Year. It takes place in September or October. For every Jew Rosh Hashanah is a period of serious thought and reflection. It ends ten days later with Yom Kippur – the Day of Atonement.

Why do you think that Rosh Hashanah is the most serious day in the Jewish year?

Rosh Hashanah is one of the most serious times in the whole Jewish calendar. Many Jews take two days out to celebrate the festival.

Beginning again

The New Year is a time for beginning again and many of the customs at Rosh Hashanah reflect this. Some people have their hair cut just before the festival and buy a new outfit to wear. Others make sure that they are wearing their best clothes for the occasion. At home, too, there are many customs. In one of them, members of the family eat an apple dipped in honey. This is to allow them to wish each other a sweet year ahead.

A time of judgement

The main symbol of Rosh Hashanah is the blowing of the ram's horn (the **shofar**) before and during the festival. This instrument can produce three different sounds. Each of them is very important. They are used to call the people to repent from their sins. They are:

Why is this family eating apples dipped in honey?

For your dictionary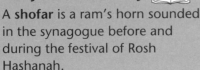

A **shofar** is a ram's horn sounded in the synagogue before and during the festival of Rosh Hashanah.

 ## Look back

Day of Atonement (page 72)
Jew (page 5)
Rosh Hashanah (page 7)
Yom Kippur (page 72)

- What is Rosh Hashanah?
- How do Jewish people celebrate Rosh Hashanah?
- What is the link between the idea of judgement and the festival of Rosh Hashanah?

- a long, drawn-out sound which calls on everyone who hears to listen

- a broken sound which reminds everyone of the Jewish people in the past who have repented for their sins

- a sharp noise which sounds like people sobbing because of their sins.

On Rosh Hashanah the shofar is blown 100 times. In the same way that trumpets are also blown to announce the coronation of a human king, the shofar is blown to announce the coronation of God. Jews everywhere are crowning Him King in their hearts. After repenting from their sins they are looking forward to a new year when they will enjoy His blessing.

An old Jewish legend (a 'midrash') says that on Rosh Hashanah three books are opened in heaven and the actions of everyone are recorded in them. The books are then sealed by God. One day everyone will be present when the books are finally opened. They will have to account for the way they have lived. It is very important, therefore, for every man and woman to seek forgiveness and a fresh start on Rosh Hashanah while they still have the opportunity.

1 This man is blowing a shofar during Rosh Hashanah. Explain what the following sounds on the shofar mean:
a   the broken sound
b   the sharp, short sound
c   the long, drawn-out sound.

2 Read this Jewish legend (midrash) about Rosh Hashanah.

'On Rosh Hashanah, three books are opened in the heavenly court; one for the wicked, one for the righteous, and one for those in between. The fate of the righteous is inscribed and sealed there and then: Life. The fate of the wicked is inscribed and sealed there and then: Death. The fate of those in between remains undecided from Rosh Hashanah to Yom Kippur. If during those days, their deeds show their worthiness, they are inscribed and sealed for Life; if not, they are inscribed and sealed for Death.'

a   Which two groups have their fates decided on Rosh Hashanah?
b   What happens to those groups?
c   Which group have a second chance?
d   How long is it between Rosh Hashanah and Yom Kippur?
e   Put this Jewish legend into your own words.

What happens on Yom Kippur?

The festival of Yom Kippur is also known as 'The Day of Atonement'. It is the holiest day in the whole Jewish year. Yom Kippur comes at the end of ten days of 'returning to God' which started on Rosh Hashanah. It is a time given over totally to prayer and fasting.

Time of prayer

Beginning after sunset on the ninth day of Rosh Hashanah, Yom Kippur is marked by 25 hours of prayer and fasting. During this time Jews make their confessions to God in public using a set form of prayers. One of the prayers used on Yom Kippur, the Ashammu ('We have abused'), works its way through the alphabet outlining all the sins that have been committed. When the letter Z is reached the worshippers know that they have been forgiven!

In fasting and praying with such intensity, Jews are simply following the example of God's angels who do not, according to Jewish tradition, either eat or drink. Instead they spend all of their time praising God. On this one day, Jews act as if they were angels.

On this day Jews follow the teaching of the Talmud which forbids:

- eating
- drinking
- washing
- sexual intercourse
- anointing the body with oil
- wearing leather shoes or sandals.

Satan and his temptations

There is a very old Jewish tradition which says that Satan, the Devil, is allowed by God to tempt the Jews on any day of the week – except Yom Kippur. On that day Satan is told by God:

How is Yom Kippur a different day to all the others in the year?

'You have no power over them today; nevertheless go and see what they are doing.'

When Satan goes, he finds all the Jews fasting and dressed like angels in white clothing. He returns to God embarrassed. He says to Him:

'They are like angels and I have no power over them.'

At this time God puts Satan into chains and tells his people:

'I have forgiven you all.'

To Jewish people Yom Kippur is therefore, above everything else, a day to seek forgiveness. That is why it is called the 'Day of Atonement'. They seek forgiveness from their relations, friends and neighbours that they have hurt or wronged. As they do this so God extends His forgiveness to them as well.

At the end of Yom Kippur a special service is held, called Neilah ('the closing of the gates'). It recalls the closing of the Temple gates in Jerusalem at sunset centuries ago. The Ark remains open throughout the service – as did the old Temple gates. The message throughout the many prayers said during Neilah is the same – that God will forgive anyone who truly repents. The people say the Shema and the shofar is sounded for a last time. The closing of the Temple gates is taken as a symbol of the gates of heaven also closing.

Blowing the shofar at the end of the Neilah service.

 Look back

- Why do Jews not eat or drink during Yom Kippur and what is this practice called?
- How do Jews seek to imitate the angels on Yom Kippur?
- Why is Yom Kippur also called the 'Day of Atonement'?

1 a What is the meaning of the Neilah service – the last service held during Yom Kippur?

b What do you think is the importance of the shofar being blown at the end of the Neilah service?

c After the shofar is blown the people in the synagogue say the words:

'Next year in Jerusalem.'

Find out the meaning and importance of these words.

2 Write two sentences about each of the following:

a Rosh Hashanah
b Yom Kippur
c Day of Atonement
d fasting.

How is Sukkot celebrated?

In ancient Israel there were three 'pilgrimage' festivals. These drew thousands of Jews, no matter where in the Roman Empire they were living, to the Temple in Jerusalem. The autumn harvest festival, **Sukkot**, was one of these festivals. At this festival Jews remembered the 40 years that the Israelites spent wandering in the wilderness after leaving Egypt in about 1200 BCE. This completed the story told at the other two festivals:

- Pesach – the journey of the Israelites out of slavery

- Shavuot – the giving of the Law to Moses on Mount Sinai.

The timing of Sukkot is very important. The keynote of the festival is rejoicing and thankfulness to God for all that he has given the Jews. It begins just five days after the repentence of Rosh Hashanah and the intense prayer and fasting of Yom Kippur. Sukkot lasts for seven days.

During Sukkot many Jewish families build their own tabernacle (shelter) in their house or garden and live in it for part of each day. Other families camp out in a shelter built in their local synagogue.

Living in the shelter for a few days reminds them of two things:

- the temporary shelters in which the Israelites lived in the desert. Just like the shelters today, those shelters were open to the sky. This meant that the people were free to receive God's blessing from above.

- the fact that life itself is fragile and no one stays alive for very long. The material things of life do not matter very much. It is very surprising to discover just how much people can manage without. Sukkot is a celebration of all that really matters in life.

The four species

If you look at the shelter in the photograph you will notice that it is decorated with fruit and branches. Sukkot is the Jewish harvest festival. There are four symbols, or species, which are particularly associated with the festival. Each of them will be very familiar to anyone living in Israel. They are:

- the 'fruit of the goodly tree' (an etrog or a citron) which looks rather like a lemon

- a palm branch

  - a bough of a leafy tree, twigs of myrtle

  - a willow branch.

Each member of the congregation brings them along to the services in Shavuot. The citron is taken in the left hand and the other species are bound together in the right and waved many times during the Sukkot services. This happens on every day of the festival except Shabbat.

All of these plants grow in Israel. All of them need a great deal of water and Sukkot takes place just before the rainy season begins in Israel. Before the festival ends, therefore, the people pray that the earth will receive all the water it needs. As the four species are waved, each worshipper is reminded that he or she receives God's blessings from all different directions.

This family is decorating a shelter for the festival of Sukkot. Why do Jewish people live in a shelter during this festival?

Look back

- Why are the sukkot (shelters) which the Jews build left open to the skies?
- Which four symbols are associated with Sukkot?
- Why do the people pray for rain during the Sukkot services?

1 a What are the four species?

b Why do people wave the four species during a Sukkot service?

2 a This festival is called Sukkot. Why?

b What is the link between this festival and the land?

c Some Jewish festivals are extremely serious, while others are very happy occasions. Into which group do you think Sukkot falls? Why?

3 Copy this paragraph into your book filling in the missing words as you go.

In ancient _____ thousands of Israelites visited the _____ in _____ each year for three _____ festivals. During _____ they remembered the journey of the _____ out of _____. At _____ the giving of the _____ to _____ on _____ _____ was recalled. When they visited the Temple for Sukkot everyone remembered the journey of _____ years which the _____ had spent in the _____ after leaving _____.

What is Simchat Torah?

Simchat Torah is also known as the Festival of the Rejoicing of the Law. It is the happiest festival in the whole Jewish year. It comes at the very end of Sukkot and lasts for just a day. It marks the beginning of the annual cycle of readings from the Torah. Jews look upon the Torah and Shabbat as God's two greatest gifts to them. The festival celebrates Jewish dedication both to God and to the Torah.

The end and the beginning

Simchat Torah marks a very important time in the life of the Jewish community. On this day the old, annual, cycle of readings from the Torah comes to an end with the last chapter of the Book of Deuteronomy. In the same service the new cycle begins with the first chapter of the Book of Genesis. It is important that the one ends and the other begins with hardly a breath being taken in-between.

The meaning of this is clear to everyone. All Jews believe that the Torah, God's Law, is eternal. It had no beginning and cannot end or pass away. As long as God's people exist so they will have the Torah. The people are expressing this truth on Simchat Torah.

Dancing with the Torah

Every Shabbat one, or maybe two, scrolls are taken out of the Ark and several chapters are read from the Torah. On Simchat Torah, however, all of the scrolls are taken out. The people in the congregation then dance around the Ark with them. They make seven journeys around the synagogue while other people follow behind – singing psalms and clapping their hands. Children kiss the scrolls, carry banners, light candles and receive sweets during the celebrations. It is a time for everyone, young and old, to be happy.

These celebrations remind everyone of a Jewish wedding. This is no coincidence. The Torah is often referred to as a 'bride' in the Jewish Scriptures. She has been given in 'marriage' by God to the Jewish people. In the wedding service the Jewish bride walks her husband seven times around the wedding canopy. In a similar way, the Torah is paraded around the synagogue – usually seven times.

These people are dancing as the scrolls of the Ark are carried around the synagogue. Why do you think the people are so happy?

The scrolls of the Torah are obviously a very important part of Jewish worship. Find out how they are made.

For your dictionary

Simchat Torah is the day on which the reading of the old cycle from the Torah ends and a new cycle begins.

 Look back

Ark (page 41)
Shabbat (page 7)
Sukkot (page 83)
Synagogue (page 5)
Torah (page 5)

- What is the Torah?
- Which is the happiest festival in the Jewish year – and when does it take place?
- Why is Simchat Torah an important Jewish festival?

1 Here are two drawings to illustrate scenes from the festival of Simchat Torah.

Produce your own drawings to illustrate these two scenes. Describe what is happening in each of your drawings.

2 Answer each of these questions in your own words.
a How long does it take for the whole of the Torah to be read in the synagogue?
b What belief about the Torah is underlined as the people celebrate Simchat Torah each year?
c How are the scrolls of the Torah treated differently on Simchat Torah compared with the rest of the year?
d Why are the scrolls of the Torah carried in front of dancing people around the synagogue seven times?
e How do Jewish children celebrate Simchat Torah?

What happens on Hanukkah?

Hanukkah is the Jewish Festival of Lights. It is celebrated for eight days at the beginning of December. Hanukkah is unique among all the Jewish festivals. It is the only festival which is not mentioned in the Scriptures. However, it looks back to a very important event in Jewish history.

In 165 BCE a Jewish army, led by Judas Maccabeus, recaptured the Temple from the Greeks. For a long time the Temple had been used by the Greeks for the worship of **Zeus**. This upset the Jews, because they believed the Temple was God's house.

When the Temple was recaptured an eight-day festival was declared. The Temple was cleansed of every Greek religious object. The old **menorah** (eight-branched candlestick) was damaged and so a temporary one was made out of the soldiers' spears. In this way the weapons of war became the agents of peace.

The miracle

In front of the Ark in the Temple stood the Everlasting Light. As its name suggests, this light was never allowed to go out. When they looked around for oil to put in the light they could only find enough for a single day. Miraculously, however, the supply lasted for eight days until more oil was found. This is the miracle that is celebrated at Hanukkah.

Celebrating Hanukkah today

The festival of Hanukkah is marked by lights and happiness. On each night of the festival another candle is lit in the menorah. By the end there are eight candles alight. The first candle, the **shamash**, is the servant candle and is used to light the rest. Each candle must be lit soon after sunset so that even the youngest member of the family can share the excitement.

There is a traditional game which is played by the whole family at Hanukkah. They play with dreidles. These are spinning tops which have Hebrew letters on each of the four sides. These letters are the initial letters of four Hebrew words which mean 'a great miracle took place there'.

Jewish families eat food cooked in oil, such as doughnuts. These remind them of the single jar of oil. They also enjoy a special chip – also cooked in oil. Presents are given and received. Little wonder that Hanukkah is the most popular festival with Jewish children.

How did the menorah become a symbol of peace when Judas Maccabeus cleansed the Temple of all Greek objects?

- What miracle forms the background to the celebrating of Hanukkah?
- What are dreidles and why do they play an important part in the celebrations of Hanukkah?
- How are people reminded of the miracle of Hanukkah through the food they eat during the festival?

What is this Jewish family playing with?

For your dictionary

A **menorah** is an eight-branched candelabra which is lit on Hanukkah.

Shamash is the first candle lit in the candelabra. It is used on later nights to light the other candles.

Zeus was the chief of the Greek gods who dwelt on Mount Olympus.

Look back

Ark (page 41)
Everlasting Light (page 49)
Hanukkah (page 72)
Hebrew (page 5)
Jew (page 5)
Scriptures (page 5)
Temple (page 15)

1 As each candle on the menorah is lit so this prayer is said:

'These lights are holy and we are not permitted to make use of them, but only to see them in order to thank Your name for the wonders, the victories, and the marvellous deeds.'

a What are the Jews not allowed to do with the menorah candles?
b What are the Jews allowed to do with the candles?
c What do the candles remind each Jewish worshipper of?

2 This passage explains the beginning of the festival of Hanukkah:

'And they built the sanctuary and the interior of the Temple and consecrated the courts. And they made new holy dishes and they brought the lampstand and the altar of incense and the table into the Temple. And they burned incense on the altar, and lighted the lamps on the lampstand and they lighted the Temple...Then Judas and his brothers and all the congregation of Israel decreed that the days of the rededication of the altar should be observed at their season, every year, for eight days...with gladness and joy.'
(1.Maccabees 4.48–59)

a Why do you think that Hanukkah is called the Festival of Lights?
b How often is the festival to be held?
c For how long does the festival last?
d In what mood are the people to celebrate?

How is Purim celebrated?

The festival of **Purim** is held in February or March. 'Purim' means 'lots' and refers to an event in Jewish history that happened over 2000 years ago. Haman, the chief minister of the Persian King, planned to destroy all the Jews in Persia. He cast lots to decide the best way to do this. The story is told in the Book of **Esther** in the Jewish Scriptures. This book is read aloud in the synagogue in services on the evening and morning of Purim.

Haman decided to kill all the Jews in Persia because one Jew, Mordecai, refused to bow down before him. On the day indicated by the lots, Haman went to King Ahasuerus to offer him a large sum of money if he would execute all the Jews. The King agreed. He sent out a proclamation (order) that all the Jews be put to death on a certain day.

Esther denouncing Haman to King Ahasuerus.

Mordecai heard of the plot and told Esther, the Queen of Persia. Esther knew that she must talk to the King, but that was a dangerous thing to do. She asked Mordecai and all the Jews to fast for three days so that she might know what God wanted her to do.

After the fast, Esther invited the King and Haman to a banquet. Haman had some gallows built so that he could execute Mordecai. However, the King discovered how Mordecai had once saved his life and so Haman could not carry out his plan. At the banquet Esther denounced Haman, and the King had him hanged on the gallows he had built for Mordecai. The King cancelled his proclamation. The whole Jewish nation was saved through the courage of one woman – Esther.

The Book of Esther in the Scriptures is the only book in which the name of God is not mentioned. But God is very much in the background, controlling what is happening. This is the theme of Purim – good will always triumph over evil.

Celebrating Purim

Jewish people fast on the day before Purim in memory of Esther's fast. During the reading of the Book of Esther in the synagogue, whenever the name of Haman is mentioned the people hiss, boo, stamp their feet, blow whistles and shake rattles! They are trying drown out his name.

Purim is a happy festival. The children perform in plays which tell the story of Esther, and go to parties. In Israel the story is retold through carnivals and processions in the streets of the main cities.

There is one unusual feature of Purim. The Persian King killed his first wife when he was drunk. If this had not happened, he would not have married Esther. Jews are usually encouraged only to drink alcohol in moderation. But on Purim the restriction is lifted a little.

The festival also has its serious side. On Purim worshippers:

* give gifts away to the poor
* send food parcels to other families.

For your dictionary

Esther was the heroine of the book in the Jewish Scriptures which carries her name. She saved Jewish people.

Purim is the Jewish festival which celebrates the saving of the Jewish people by Mordecai and Esther.

Look back

Hanukkah (page 72)
Scriptures (page 5)
Synagogue (page 5)

- What is unusual about the Book of Esther in the Jewish Scriptures?
- What is the theme behind the festival of Purim?
- Why are Jewish people encouraged to get drink a lot of alcohol on the festival of Purim?

These children are stamping their feet in the synagogue on Purim. Whose name do you think they have written on the soles of their feet?

1 Here is a prayer which is said on Purim:

'We thank you for the wonders, for the heroic acts, for the victories, for the marvellous and consoling deeds which you performed for our fathers in those days at this season. In the days of Mordecai and Esther, in Shushan the capital, when the wicked Haman rose up against them, he sought to destroy, kill and exterminate all Jews, both young and old, little children and women, on one day and plunder their possessions...then you, in your great mercy, upset his plan and overthrew his design and made his acts recoil upon his own head...'

a How does the reason for Purim remind you of the reason of Hanukkah?

b Who were Mordecai, Esther and Haman?

c What did Haman intend to do to the Jews?

d How did God make the acts of Haman 'recoil upon his own head'?

2 These children are at a Purim service. Why do you think they are dressed up?

How do Jews prepare for Pesach?

The most important Jewish festival of all is Pesach (also known as Passover). This festival commemorates two crucial events in Jewish history:

- the deliverance of the Israelites from their slavery in Egypt (the Exodus). No event in Jewish history shows more clearly the power of God. It was God who made it possible for the Israelites to leave Egypt. By so doing he clearly showed His concern for the Jews and his willingness to rescue them from their enemies.

- the journey of the Israelites across the wilderness towards the Promised Land of Canaan. During this time the Jews received the Torah from the hand of God when Moses climbed Mount Sinai.

These events took place around 1200 BCE. Every part of the Pesach celebrations is intended to help Jews to re-live them. Jews must be able to feel as if they were actually there – as the slaves left Egypt.

God told the Israelites that they were to celebrate their deliverance from Egypt by holding an annual festival. During this festival they were not to eat, or even to have in their houses, any yeast. When the Israelites left Egypt they did so in a hurry. They did not even have time to take any leaven with them for their cooking. (Leaven is a substance like yeast that makes bread rise.) To remind them of their swift deliverance Jews only eat that food which is leaven-free (or 'unleavened') during Pesach.

To remove all yeast from the house involves a total spring-clean before the festival begins. In modern Jewish homes this often takes the form of a game which involves the whole family. Leaven is hidden around the house by the mother and the children have to find it. More seriously, all drawers and cupboards are cleaned out. The cooker and sink are thoroughly cleaned. All eating and cooking utensils are washed. In many homes new utensils are brought out for Pesach.

The game is making an important point. We know that when the Israelites left Egypt, they did so in such a hurry that they did not have time to take any yeast with them. This meant that they could only eat flat loaves (**matzah**) during their 40 years in the wilderness. This is an experience which all modern Jews try to share. They do not use any yeast in their cooking while Pesach is going on.

- Which two events in Jewish history are in people's minds as they celebrate Pesach?
- What is leaven and why are Jewish people to avoid all contact with it during Pesach?
- How does a Jewish family prepare for Pesach?

This father is about to hide a piece of leaven somewhere in the house. Why does this form an important part of the Pesach celebration?

On the day before Pesach begins, the special **Seder** meal is prepared. The table is laid. Every item on the table is there for a reason. As we shall see on page 92, its purpose is to remind everyone of the great price which was paid by every slave in Egypt. It may have happened a long time ago, but the deliverance from slavery was the most important event in Jewish history. It remains so today for every Jewish man and woman.

For your dictionary

The **Hagadah** is the prayer book which is used for the Seder service on the eve of Pesach.
Matzah (plural **matzot**) is the unleavened bread (made without yeast) which is eaten during the eight days of Pesach.
Seder means 'order'. It is the service which is followed at the meal which opens Pesach.

Look back

Canaan (page 9)
Exodus (page 13)
Israelites (page 5)
Jew (page 5)
Moses (page 5)
Mount Sinai (page 13)
Pesach (page 7)
Promised Land (page 11)
Torah (page 5)

1 a The table is ready for the Seder meal. Explain what the word 'Seder' means.
b Name three foods that you can see on the table. You will find out why they are there on page 92.

2 During the Pesach meal these words are read:

'In every generation everyone should regard himself as if he had personally come out of Egypt.' (From the Seder service, the **Hagadah**)

a Why do you think that everyone at the meal is encouraged to try to imagine what it was really like coming out of Egypt?
b How do you think they set about doing this?

How do Jews celebrate Pesach?

Pesach is an eight-day spring festival. The Hagadah (telling) is a story book which is used at the Pesach Seder meal. The book helps Jews to look back to the departure of the Jews from Egypt. It is also updated with references and examples drawn from every generation. It underlines the emphasis in the festival on freedom – freedom in the past from slavery, freedom in the present and freedom in the future. The lesson of the Exodus from Egypt is that everyone should be free.

On the eve of Pesach, the men in the family attend a special service in the synagogue. They then return home to eat and drink the Seder meal.

The Seder meal

The Seder meal begins with the drinking of four glasses of wine. These are reminders of the four promises that God made to Moses. In front of the family on the table there are a number of symbolic items to help them to recreate the events of over 3000 years ago. Two of these items are not eaten:

- a roasted shank-bone. Until 70 CE a lamb was slaughtered every year in the Temple in Jerusalem. The Temple was then destroyed by the Romans. It was never replaced and animal sacrifice died with it. The shank-bone reminds worshippers of this.

- a roast egg. This also recalls animal sacrifices in the Temple.

These two items recall religious practices which have long since stopped.

The other items on the table are tasted:

- three matzot loaves of unleavened bread

- maror, or bitter herbs, to recall the bitterness of slavery in Egypt

- a green vegetable, usually parsley, which is dipped into salt water. This is a reminder of the tears that the Israelite slaves cried in captivity

- haroset – a mixture of nuts, wine and apples – which is a reminder of the cement that the Jews used to build houses for their Egyptian masters.

A fifth cup of wine stands on the table but no one drinks it. Jewish tradition says that the old prophet Elijah will come back to earth. This will be before the Messiah comes.

The four questions

The Seder meal follows a careful pattern. The different courses are interspersed with readings from the Scriptures. The service is laid down in the Hagadah. During the meal the youngest person at the table asks four questions. You can find out what these are on the opposite page.

Why do you think that Jews use these foods to help them to remember the Exodus?

Why do you think the youngest person in the family is chosen to ask questions about the meaning of Pesach?

- What do the four glasses of wine drunk at the Seder meal remind people about?
- Which two items of food on the Seder table are not eaten? Why not?
- Which four items of food on the table are eaten? What do they remind the people about?

 Look back

1 Four promises were made by God to Moses. The Seder service reminds everyone about them:

'Say therefore to the people of Israel, "I am the Lord and I will bring you out from under their bondage, and I will redeem you with an outstretched arm and with great acts of judgement, I will take you for my people, and I will be your God."' (From the Seder service, the Hagadah)

a What are the four promises that God made to Moses?
b How do the worshippers remind themselves of these promises during the Seder meal?

2 The youngest person around the Seder table asks four questions after wondering:

'Why is this night different from all other nights?' (From the Seder service, the Hagadah)

The four questions are:

1 *'To-night why do we only eat eat matzot?'*
2 *'To-night why do we eat bitter herbs?'*
3 *'To-night why do we dip twice?'*
4 *'To-night why do we lean [as we eat]?'*

Find out the answers to questions 1, 2 and 3.

What happens on Shavuot?

The festival of Shavuot (Pentecost) is also known as the Feast of Weeks because it comes seven weeks after Pesach. Like Sukkot, this summer festival is associated with the harvest time in the country of Israel. It looks back to the time when God gave Moses the Law (Torah) on Mount Sinai. Jews look upon the Torah as God's greatest gift to them.

Centuries ago, during harvest festival, all Jewish farmers brought their 'first fruits' (the first crops harvested) to the Temple. They offered them as a token of their thankfulness to God. As they did so, they thanked God for giving them the Promised Land, Canaan, a land 'flowing with milk and honey' to farm. Today synagogues are beautifully decorated with plants, fruits and flowers for Shavuot. This is a reminder that the normally barren Mount Sinai burst into fruit in preparation for the giving of the Torah to Moses. It also recalls the harvest origins of this festival.

Today, however, it is the giving of the Law, rather than harvest, which is most important at Shavuot.

No event in their history is more important to a Jew. Ever since God gave Moses the Torah on Mount Sinai, Jews have tried to live by the many laws which God gave to them. The same Torah continues to have an enormous influence on the way that Jews live their lives today.

Shavuot today

On the evening before Shavuot Jews stay up all night to read and study the Torah. They keep themselves awake by drinking large amounts of coffee and eating dairy produce – especially cheesecake. Honeycake is also a traditional Shavuot food – to remind everyone that the Torah is sweet to the spiritual taste.

Apart from reading the Torah, Jews also read the book of **Ruth** on Shavuot. This is a beautiful love story from the Jewish Scriptures. It tells how Ruth was converted to the Jewish faith after helping her husband's family gather in the year's harvest. This makes it a very appropriate reading for this time of the year.

In Israel, the festival coincides with the gathering in of the harvest. Farmers bring baskets of bikkurim (ripe first fruits) to a central area. By doing this they are expressing their thankfulness to God for the fruitfulness of the land which has fed their ancestors for centuries. They remind themselves that it is still a land 'flowing with milk and honey'.

* What is the link between the festival of Shavuot and harvest festival?
* What very important event in Jewish history happened on Mount Sinai?
* How do Jewish people celebrate the festival of Shavuot today?

Why do you think that Jewish farmers were expected to bring the 'first fruits' of their harvest to the Temple?

Why do you think that the tradition is for those working on the land to present their 'first-fruits' to God? What is so special about the first of the harvest that is gathered in?

For your dictionary

Ruth was a Gentile (non-Jew) who was married to a Jew.

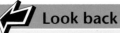 **Look back**

1 These words come from the Jewish Scriptures:

'You shall also count for yourselves from the day after the sabbath "the end of the Passover", from the day when you brought in the sheaf of the wave offering; there shall be seven complete sabbaths. You shall count fifty days to the day after the seventh sabbath; then you shall present a new grain offering to the Lord.' (Leviticus 23.15–16)

a How long after the end of Pesach must pass before the festival of Shavuot is celebrated?
b What are Jews told to do on the festival of Shavuot?

2 In this crossword you have the answers but no clues. Write out your own one-sentence clues to go with the answers.

```
                S
                H
            C A N A A N
                V
    B I K K U R I M
                O
H A R V E S T O R A H
    U
    T
    H
```

Index

Page references in bold indicate that the word is defined on this page in the 'For your dictionary' box.